BUSINESS AND ECONOMICS RESEARCH SERIES

General Editor: Professor Dermot McAleese (Trinity College, Dublin)

Competition and Industry
Ireland's Changing Demographic Structure
Small Firm Competitiveness and Performance
Privatisation: Issues of Principle and Implementation in Ireland

Forthcoming:

Making the Irish Labour Market Work
Overseas Industry in Ireland

TRANSPORT POLICY IN IRELAND IN THE 1990s

Seán D. Barrett

Gill and Macmillan

Published in Ireland by
Gill and Macmillan Ltd
Goldenbridge
Dublin 8

with associated companies in
Auckland, Delhi, Gaborone, Hamburg, Harare,
Hong Kong, Johannesburg, Kuala Lumpur, Lagos, London,
Manzini, Melbourne, Mexico City, Nairobi,
New York, Singapore, Tokyo

© Seán D. Barrett 1991

Designed by The Unlimited Design Company, Dublin

Print origination by Seton Music Graphics, Co. Cork

Printed by
Colour Books Ltd, Dublin

British Library Cataloguing in Publication Data
A CIP catalogue record for this book
is available from the British Library

0 7171 1678 6

To Geraldine Barrett

Contents

F Foreword by the Minister for Tourism and Transport, Séamus Brennan TD

P Preface

FOREWORD

by the Minister for Tourism and Transport,
Séamus Brennan TD

I congratulate Dr Barrett on his interesting assessment of Irish transport policy in the coming decades. As an island nation, Ireland must regard transport as a critical activity to the functioning and development of every aspect of its economy. The imminence of the Single European Market and the integration of our economy with continental Europe gives transport issues an even higher priority. To compete with other producers on an equal basis in the new Europe, Irish exporters must be in a position to ensure that their products reach the consumer quickly, efficiently, and cost-competitively. A sound approach to the management of the transport infrastructure will be one of the deciding factors in determining the degree of success or failure of the Irish economy in the 1990s.

In planning the transport needs of our economy, the Government has made a strong case to the EC for assistance with a wide range of integrated developments to redress the natural imbalance Ireland suffers because of its peripheral location and island status. We are confident that aid from the EC Structural Funds, coupled with domestic private and public investment, will ameliorate if not eliminate the natural disadvantages with which Ireland begins the decade.

Dr Seán Barrett has always been an imaginative contributor to transport policy in Ireland, adding his opinions to every public debate and controversy on transport issues. I may not agree with all of his views, but there is no doubt that everyone interested in the development and enhanced management of the transport sector appreciates his commitment. I welcome both the freshness of his viewpoints and the vigorous style in which he propounds them.

PREFACE

Irish transport policy has undergone radical change in recent years, after a long period of remarkably little change following anti-competitive legislation in 1932 and 1933.

Spectacular growth followed the deregulation of Anglo-Irish air services in 1986. The deregulation of road haulage also brought significant expansion and changed traditional market shares. Bus deregulation is about to be introduced, and has in any case existed de facto for most of the 1980s.

Concern with the social costs of transport is probably greater than ever, while the attempts to solve the problems of Ireland's public finances will require strict expenditure appraisal of transport investments and subsidies. This book is intended to bring forward the issues discussed in *Transport Policy in Ireland* (1982) and to incorporate recent and probable policy changes.

I thank the students of Trinity College, Dublin, for their enthusiastic interest in transport economics. I am indebted to my colleagues at the Department of Economics, and in particular to Professor Dermot McAleese, editor of this series. Mr Brian MacIntyre was an enthusiastic research assistant, and Mr Conor Mitton read the typescript. Kevin Carey also provided valuable assistance, and Margaret Lawlor typed the manuscript with great efficiency. I am grateful to them all, but I am responsible for any errors that remain.

THE REGULATION OF AVIATION

The postwar regulation of aviation by governments, and collusive behaviour by airlines, had many anti-competitive aspects, such as exclusion of new entrants from the market, price collusion between national airlines, and market sharing with a predetermined market size agreed between the airlines of each country. The European Civil Aviation Conference noted (ECAC, 1981, p. 11) that 'airlines enter into inter-airline agreements which formalise the above arrangements and also provide for each airline to act as the other's agent for their aspects such as baggage and cargo handling, reservations and ticket sales and also for pooling and sharing the revenue obtained from the operation of routes.' In Europe, restrictions on competition in aviation were historically supported by all governments, with the exception of Britain and the Netherlands. Europe's air fares became the highest in the world according to the annual surveys of the International Civil Aviation Organisation (ICAO), and were substantially above the level in North America. The 1985 survey, for example, stated that 'average "local Europe" fares remain among the highest in the world at shorter distances; in September 1985 they were 26% higher than the world average at 250 km and 18% higher than the world average at 500 km.' Only at 4,000 km did the European fares fall below the world average; but these routes accounted for only 0.2 per cent of the 2,310 routes in the ICAO survey. Table 1 shows the results of the ICAO survey in 1977 and 1985.

International aviation policy in the postwar period was based on three barriers to competition. New entrants were forbidden; tariffs were fixed by the airlines in advance; and capacity was shared between airlines. Table 2 shows the options in liberalising European aviation by dismantling these barriers to competition. The postwar movement to free trade in industrial goods did not begin to affect aviation until the mid-1980s. Aviation was not included in the General Agreement on Tariffs and Trade (GATT) and was given de facto exemption from the competition policy of the European Community. The airlines' trade association was allowed to operate as a cartel, and govern-

Table 1

European, North American and international air fares, 1977–85, per passenger-kilometre (US cents)

DISTANCE (km)	250	500	1,000	2,000	4,000
		1977			
Europe	21.9	17.5	14.1	11.3	10.1
North America	12.1	9.4	7.4	5.3	4.5
World average	16.9	14.3	12.2	10.4	8.8
		1985			
Europe	36.3	27.9	21.5	16.6	12.8
North America	25.3	19.1	14.4	10.9	8.2
World average	28.7	23.6	19.4	16.0	13.2
Index 1977 (world = 100)					
Europe	129	122	116	109	115
North America	79	66	61	51	51
Index 1985 (world = 100)					
Europe	126	118	111	104	96 *
North America	88	81	74	68	62

*This group accounted for only 0.2 per cent of the 2,310 European air routes in the ICAO survey.
Source: Annual Survey of International Air Transport Fares and Rates, International Civil Aviation Authority, Montreal.

ments were examples of regulatory capture by national airlines in the producer interest.

THE COMPETITIVE ALTERNATIVE
During the era of tight regulation of aviation in the interest of existing airlines, there were a number of examples of competitive markets. In the United States, while the market for interstate air travel was tightly controlled from 1938 to 1978, these federal

Table 2

Options in liberalising European aviation

COMBINATION	REGULATION OF ROUTE ENTRY	TARIFFS	CAPACITY	TITLE
A	Yes	Yes	Yes	Present system.
B	No	Yes	Yes	Bilateral with regulation of tariffs/capacity. New entrants allowed.
C	Yes	No	Yes	Bilateral with regulation of route entry/capacity. Price competition.
D	Yes	Yes	No	Bilateral with regulation of route entry/capacity. Capacity competition.
E	No	Yes	No	Bilateral with tariff regulation only.
F	Yes	No	No	Bilateral with route entry regulation only.
G	No	No	No	Bilateral competition.
H	No	No	No	Multilateral competition.

Source: Adapted from ECAC (1981), table 5.1.

regulations on entry did not apply within states. The divergence between fares within California and Texas and those controlled by the federal government brought into question whether regulation was in the interests of the producers or the public. Jordan (1970) estimated that 'during late 1965 the coach fares in the major California markets were as much as 47 per cent lower than they would have been under CAB [Civil Aeronautics Board] policies and authorisations.'

In Europe the promotion of tourism led to the growth of charter airlines, which attained over 40 per cent of the passenger market within the region. The ECAC 'Compass Report' (1981) found that 'most member states, irrespective of their approach towards the regulation of scheduled services, have a comparatively liberal approach towards the regulation of non-scheduled operations ... The only or primary objective in relation to non-scheduled operations seems to be the transportation of passengers and the development of tourism.' Within Europe, charter airlines were acceptable to Spain, Greece, Italy, Portugal, and France, which supported the restraint of competition in scheduled aviation.

The 'Cascade Studies' (EC, 1981) compared the fares charged by British Airways and British charter airlines, and found that actual charter fares were between 32 and 37 per cent of the scheduled airline fares. The scheduled airlines could have produced a 'charter-type' service for between 36 and 39 per cent of their scheduled fares. The alleged inferiority of the charter product included higher load factors and seat density, lower standards of service, and more night flying. The result of the Cascade Studies is shown in table 3.

The scheduled airlines' defence against the lower fares charged by the charter airlines, and the fact that the scheduled carriers could virtually match these fares if they wished, raised important questions about whether Europe's national airlines had misjudged the market by deciding not to produce the charter-type product, and whether in fact there was any great margin of superior service in Europe's high-fare scheduled services over the low-fare charter product.

The evidence that Europe's scheduled airlines charged too much compared with world and US fares, and compared with the charter airlines operating in the same European cost environment, strengthened interest in opening up Europe's closed

Table 3

The 'Cascade' analysis of the costs of scheduled and charter airlines in Europe

CASCADE STEPS	ROUTE A	ROUTE B	ROUTE C
TOTAL SCHEDULED COST PER PASSENGER	100	100	100
1. Deduct commission	92	92	91
2. Tourist class	86	84	87
3. Seating density	77	80	83
4. Load factor	56	59	60
5. Peak/trough ratio	60	62	63
6. Utilisation	57	60	61
7. Standards	51	51	53
8. Not applicable	36	37	39
Derived 'charter'	36	37	39
Actual charter	34–37	32	35

Note: In the table the fare difference between scheduled and chartered airlines is attributed to differences in service standards such as seat pitch, load factor, lower service standards, etc. *The scheduled airlines could produce a charter-type product for between 36 and 39 per cent of their present fares, thus almost matching the charter airlines, which charge between 32 and 37 per cent of the scheduled airlines' fares.* The Cascade Studies, commissioned to defend Europe's scheduled airlines, indicate their choice of a high-cost strategy.

Source: EC (1981).

scheduled aviation markets. Three important liberalisations took place in the years 1982–86: the relaxation of the barriers to market forces in the 1982–84 internal liberalisation of the major domestic British trunk routes; the 1984 Anglo-Dutch agreement; and the Anglo-Irish deregulation of 1986.

THE BRITISH TRUNK ROUTE LIBERALISATIONS (1982–84)

In October 1982 British Midland entered the Glasgow–Heathrow route; it began the Edinburgh–Heathrow route in March l983, and the Belfast–Heathrow route in April 1984. The Civil Aviation Authority (CAA) paper *Competition on the Main Domestic Trunk Routes* (1987) found rapid growth in the year of entry of a second operator at Heathrow, particularly in 1983 and 1984 for the Glasgow and Edinburgh routes, and 1984 for Belfast. Growth then slackened. 'This suggests that additional service at Heathrow may have provided a sharp stimulus to traffic but with no prolonged effect on long term traffic growth' (p. 55).

On fares there was an initial reduction in economy, but by 1986 'the economy fares on all routes were higher in real terms than in April 1980 and British Midland's economy fares were up to the same level as those of British Airways' (p. 55). Promotional fares such as APEX fell by 30 per cent on the Glasgow and Edinburgh routes and by 16 to 22 per cent on the Belfast route.

THE ANGLO-DUTCH LIBERALISATION OF 1984

From 1 July 1984 any airline based in Britain or the Netherlands could fly between them at fares determined by the country of origin. Decisions on frequency and capacity were made by the airlines, which were also free to match any fares set by competitors. Airlines have pricing freedom unless both governments disapprove. Ten new services were introduced in the first year. Whereas there was no growth in the number of passengers carried in this market between 1976 and 1983, there was a growth of 21.3 per cent in 1985.

The OECD report *Deregulation and Airline Competition* (1988) found that the liberalisation did not reduce the economy fare until British Midland entered the route in 1986, at a fare of £138 return on the London–Amsterdam route compared with £170 by British Airways, British Caledonian, KLM, and Transavia. On the other hand the lowest promotional fare declined from 59 per cent of the economy fare before liberalisation to 23 per cent after liberalisation.

On traffic numbers, the OECD compared Dutch and French traffic growth from Britain over the years 1980–86. Before the Anglo-Dutch liberalisation, growth on these routes lagged behind the French routes, but after 1983 it became 'considerably faster' (p. 59). The growth increased by between 3 and 5 per cent per year because of the liberalised air services agreement with the Netherlands.

THE ANGLO-IRISH LIBERALISATION OF 1986

Between 1978 and 1985 air travel between Ireland and Britain declined by 6 per cent. Liberalisation took place in 1986 with the entry of Ryanair to the market previously dominated by Aer Lingus and British Airways. Virgin Atlantic entered the market in June 1987, and British Midland in April 1989. Capital Airlines replaced Virgin Atlantic in August 1989.

The CAA's analysis of eleven major routes over the years 1980–85, including London–Dublin, is shown in table 4. London–Dublin had by far the lowest traffic growth, at 2.8 per cent over the five years, compared with 58.3 per cent for London–Edinburgh and 29.9 per cent average growth for the eleven routes.

The London–Dublin fares increase was the highest, at 72.6 per cent, compared with Aberdeen, the lowest, at 29.2 per cent and the average of 43.7 per cent. The retail price index for the UK over the period was 41.5 per cent. The Dublin route was also characterised by the highest load factor, at 75.2 compared with an average of 65.5. The Dublin route also had a lower than average proportion of business travellers and lower than average interlining in London (i.e. travelling to another destination by air from London).

The largest fare reductions in the years following liberalisation occurred for those on unrestricted fares (table 5). The savings ranged from 41 per cent to 66 per cent of the £208 fare charged by the incumbent airlines. In response Aer Lingus introduced a hotel voucher worth up to £95 sterling. This was called the 'London Business Bonus' and was introduced for the passenger from Ireland to London. Excursion fares were cut by 34 and 35 per cent for APEX tickets and by 44 per cent for tickets that required a Saturday night away.

Table 6 combines the estimated savings for unrestricted and restricted fares, based on market information before and after the deregulation of fares. It is estimated that the total savings for the existing traffic were £24.9 million or 31 per cent. The saving per passenger-journey was £25.

In valuing the benefits from a change in resource allocation it is customary to use a value of one half for the units of generated traffic compared with existing traffic. The growth of 107

Table 4

London–Dublin and major routes from London compared, 1980–85

London to—	PASSENGER NOS. 1985 (000)	LOAD FACTOR 1985	FARE INCREASE 1980–85 (%)	PASSENGER GROWTH 1980–85 (%)	BUSINESS SHARE (%)	INTER-LINE (%)
Glasgow	1,080.8	62.6	31.9	40.4	72	25
Edinburgh	1,033.9	62.7	31.9	58.3	63	34
Belfast	895.3	60.8	40.9	30.7	44	18
Manchester	869.1	59.8	45.5	41.9	79	44
Aberdeen	460.3	64.6	29.2	34.5	69	33
Newcastle	313.2	58.0	38.8	18.4	73	42
Paris	2,438.3	73.9	63.2	17.1	57	15
Amsterdam	1,312.5	70.8	38.5	24.1	57	13
Dublin	994.3	75.2	72.6	2.8	45	25
Frankfurt	977.4	70.6	43.2	40.1	58	19
Brussels	719.0	61.7	43.6	20.4	68	31
Average (11)		65.5	43.7	29.9	62	30

Fare comparison note: retail price index increase 1980–85: 41.5%.
Interline data refers to interlining in London, i.e. travelling to another destination by air via London.

Source: CAA (1987).

Note: London–Dublin indices as proportion of eleven major routes from London (average = 100)

Passenger growth	1980–85	9
Fare increase	1980–85	166
Load factor	1985	115
Business travellers (%)	1985	73
London interlining (%)	1985	83

Source: Derived from main table above.

Dublin–London fares before and after deregulation (£IR)

	SUMMER 1988	BEFORE MAY 1986	FARE RE-DUCTION (%)
NEW ENTRANTS			
Virgin Atlantic one-way peak	38	91 *	58
Ryanair one-way peak	54	91 *	41
Virgin Atlantic off-peak	35	91 *	62
Ryanair off-peak	44	91 *	52
Virgin Atlantic round trip	70–76	208 *	66–63
Ryanair round trip	88–108	208 *	58–48
ESTABLISHED CARRIERS			
(i) Restricted fares			
Maxi-saver (28-day APEX)	63	95	34
Late saver	69	no fare	—
Special saver	75	no fare	—
APEX (14-day)	77	119	35
Excursion (Saturday night away)	89	159	44
Super Budget	123	no fare	—
(ii) Unrestricted fares			
Budget (Gatwick)	164 †	164	68 †
Budget (Heathrow)	188 †	188	60 †
Executive	208 †	208	54 †
Budget one-way (Gatwick)	82	82	0
Budget one-way (Heathrow)	94	94	0
Executive one-way	104	104	0

* Comparable fare available on established carriers before May 1986.

† London Business Bonus applies. This entitles passengers at these fares to a hotel voucher in London worth up to £112 (£95 stg). Other incentives include a day's free car hire, free airport car parking, and complimentary duty-free goods or shopping vouchers.

£1IR = £0.85 sterling = $1.45.

Table 6	Estimated average yield per passenger-journey on Dublin–London route (£IR)	
REGULATION		**£**
Unrestricted fare		104
Discounted fare		62
Weighted average		81
DEREGULATION		
Established airlines unrestricted		79
Established airlines discounted		42
New airlines		47
Weighted average		56

Note: Market shares assumed are 55% unrestricted fares and 45% discounted fares under regulation. Under deregulation these proportions are retained, but the established airlines' share is reduced to 75% to accommodate the new entrants. The average benefit from deregulation to pre-deregulation traffic is therefore £25 per passenger-journey and £24.9 million in total for the 994,000 passengers. As a proportion of pre-deregulation fares the saving is 31%.

per cent in traffic between 1985 and 1988 therefore means that the benefit to generated traffic from deregulation was £12.5 million in 1988. The total benefit to consumers was therefore £36.4 million.

In 1989 the number of passengers between Dublin and London increased by a further 15 per cent to 2.3 million, i.e. 2.3 times the pre-deregulation traffic in 1985. In 1989 therefore the benefits to the generated traffic were £16.2 million for the 1.3 million extra passengers. When added to the existing traffic fare savings of £24.9 million this gives total fare savings in 1989 of £41.1 million.

Consumer prices increased over the period 1986–89 by 10 per cent in Ireland and 18 per cent in the UK. The fall in real fares under deregulation contrasts with an increase by 75 per cent more than the UK retail price index during the years 1980–85, as shown in table 4. In real terms, therefore, fares from

Britain to Ireland have fallen by 42 per cent and from Ireland to Britain by 37 per cent. The first overall increase in fares since deregulation was in the spring of 1990.

THE MARKET STRUCTURE UNDER REGULATION AND DEREGULATION

Table 7 compares the monthly increase in Dublin–London traffic under regulation in 1985 and deregulation in 1987. The largest increase took place in August (91.7 per cent), when the market share of the new entrants was highest (24.1 per cent). The established airlines used yield maximisation programmes to reduce periods of peak demand by reducing the availability of discounted fares. The new airlines did not operate these systems, and thus facilitated the expansion of the market.

SERVICE STANDARDS

The entry of British Midland to the market in April 1989 brought important benefits to users. Alone of the new entrants, it had access to Heathrow, and its three-day business fare of £123 was a saving of 41 per cent on the £208 fare charged by the established airlines on the Dublin–Heathrow route. British Midland also raised service standards, with meal service for all passengers regardless of class of ticket. This was immediately matched by Aer Lingus.

THE REGIONAL AIRPORTS IN IRELAND

Since deregulation, regional airports with international service have opened at Knock, Galway, Waterford, Kerry, Sligo, and Donegal. The new regional airports had an estimated 280,000 passengers on British routes in 1989. Cork and Shannon increased their British route traffic by 82 per cent and 113 per cent, respectively, between 1986 and 1989. The regional airports combined had 370,000 passengers to Britain in 1985 and 987,000 in 1989, an increase of 167 per cent. This compares with an increase of 108 per cent on the routes from Dublin to Britain.

The success of airline deregulation between Britain and Ireland occurred because both countries shared a market-oriented view of aviation, which led to the 1986 change of policy, and because both countries had airlines outside the traditional collusive companies. The new carriers availed of deregulation to enter new routes with lower fares than previously charged.

Table 7	Dublin–London passenger numbers under regulation and deregulation		
	1985	1987	INCREASE (%)
January	63.2	87.4	38.2
February	59.4	89.0	49.9
March	80.8	108.4	34.2
April	76.93	124.0	62.3
May	82.0	118.4	44.4
June	92.3	147.0	59.3
July	97.2	177.6	82.7
August	106.7	204.5	91.7
September	93.3	168.7	80.8
October	85.3	157.6	84.7
November	75.8	122.3	61.4
December	78.9	130.7	65.7
Year	991.7	1635.5	64.9

NEW AIRLINES' SHARE OF DUBLIN–LONDON TRAFFIC, 1987

	SHARE (%)
January	12.9
February	13.5
March	14.0
April	14.1
May	14.5
June*	21.7
July	23.4
August	24.1
September	23.2
October	22.5
November	21.8
December	20.7

* Second new entrant to market.

Source: CAA, Monthly Airport Statistics.

The Anglo-Irish policy changes in 1986 were agreed bilaterally by the British and Irish governments. No other EC country has negotiated the same type of liberal bilateral agreement with Ireland. A much slower regime of market liberalisation has been operated by the EC, with less spectacular results than between Ireland and Britain. By the end of 1992 a totally deregulated aviation market in Europe will include rights of 'cabotage' or flying between airports within another member-state, freedom of access and pricing on all routes, and the determination of capacity by consumer preference rather than by airline agreement. Machinery should also be in force for the application of competition policy to the aviation sector.

EC POLICY ON LIBERALISATION OF AVIATION
In 1979 the EC Commission proposed the application of the Treaty of Rome to air transport. The measures proposed included permitting new entrants to the aviation market where it could be shown that their proposed services would be profitable and their fare reductions significant. Where an airline (with the approval of its government) sought to introduce a new service, a new fare, or a marketing innovation, the receiving country would (after a period of consultation) no longer be able to reject the new service except on nondiscriminatory grounds such as environmental factors or congestion at airports. The Commission proposed decontrol of services by smaller aircraft. The report *Air Transport: a Community Approach* (EC, 1979, p. 14) also stated that 'in a normal industrial sector, competition on price or quality exerts a pressure on commercially managed enterprises towards greater productivity. This principle should also be true generally for air transport.'

In the years after 1979 those opposed to airline competition prevented the liberalisation of European aviation as suggested by the Commission. Opposition came from the European Parliament Transport Committee and the Economic and Social Committee, the EC social partners (Barrett, 1987, p. 15–16).

CIVIL AVIATION MEMORANDUM NO. 2
In March 1984 (EC, 1984) the Commission promised to 'maintain the structure of the present regulatory system based on bilateral intergovernmental agreements and inter-airline competition but to introduce changes to make it more flexible and more

competitive in order to increase airline efficiency, allow the efficient and innovative airline to benefit, encourage expansion and thus employment, and better meet consumer needs.'

Annex 3 of the memorandum proposed to exempt airlines from competition policy until 1991, subject to certain qualifications. Governments should not interfere to change capacity on a route in a way that guaranteed their own airlines more than 25 per cent of the business. Countries initiating fare changes would be allowed to implement them if both governments failed to agree. Revenue pool transfers would be limited to 1 per cent of poolable revenue. State subsidies were ruled out for operating losses but they could be used for restructuring. The Commission proposed that aircraft of no more than twenty-five seats would be exempt from restrictions on market entry and that 15 per cent of seats on charter services would be sold on a 'seat only' basis.

Memorandum No. 2 also proposed 'zones of reasonableness', defined as 'a pricing range within which airlines can freely establish their tariffs without seeking government approval'.

Doganis described Memorandum No. 2 as 'far-reaching, and if implemented, would dramatically change the regulatory environment for intra-Community air transport.' On the other hand Memorandum No. 2 exempted airlines from competition policy, retained the ban on new entrants to the market in aviation, and accepted price competition in only a limited way. Nevertheless the memorandum was opposed by most member-states.

REGIONAL AIR SERVICES

In 1980 the Commission proposed the deregulation of air services between regional centres in aircraft of 130 seats and under. The services proposed would exclude category 1 airports (the top 60 per cent in terms of passenger numbers in each country) and services between category 1 and category 2 airports (which accounted for the next 30 per cent of passengers). These exclusions were to 'ensure that the existing main air transport services are only marginally affected'.

The Directive on Inter-regional Air Services took effect in October 1984. It permitted regional air services subject to the following conditions:
(1) services must be between airports more than 400 km apart, or over water or other natural obstacles;

(2) the aircraft used must have fewer than seventy seats or weigh less than 30 tonnes on take-off;

(3) the service must not use a category 1 airport; and

(4) there must be no existing indirect service between any airports within 50 km at either end of the new service where total transit time is less than 90 minutes and total flight time is less than 150 per cent of the new service.

In Britain the National Consumer Council (1986, p. 58) found that 'unfortunately, but not surprisingly, very few new services have resulted from this directive, and its impact on intra-EEC services has been small. It does, however, provide a radically different route structure for those few services that can operate under its conditions.' An example is the Maersk Air service between Billund and Southend.

THE DECEMBER 1987 POLICY PACKAGE

On **fares** the EC decided in 1987 that 'Member States shall approve air fares if they are reasonably related to the long-term fully allocated costs of the applicant air carrier, while taking into account other relevant factors. In this connection they shall consider return on capital, the competitive market situation, including the need to prevent dumping. However, the fact that a proposed air fare is lower than that offered by another carrier operating on the route shall not be sufficient reason for withholding approval' (EC, 1987, article 3). Article 7 provided for an arbitration procedure in the event of a dispute between two states. Article 5 provided for a discount zone of 90 to 65 per cent of the reference fare and a deep-discount zone of 65 to 45 per cent.

On **capacity sharing** it was decided that between 1 January 1988 and 30 September 1989 capacity sharing arrangements could change from 50/50 to 55/45, and thereafter to 60/40.

On **multiple designation** it was decided that member-states should accept multiple designation on a country-pair basis but would not be obliged to accept multiple designation on any route below 250,000 passengers in the first year, 200,000 passengers in the second year, and 180,000 passengers in the third year. The multiple designation would form part of the capacity share of the country in which the airline was based.

The December 1987 agreement also provided for 'fifth-freedom' rights, for example the carriage of passengers between Britain and continental Europe by Irish airlines. Ireland and

Portugal were allowed to operate these fifth-freedom services between category 1 airports as a concession, while the other states must have at least one of the airports outside category 1. Fifth-freedom services are only allowed to use one-third of capacity for fifth-freedom passengers.

Under the December 1987 package, aviation is given block exemptions from EC competition policy until 31 January 1991 for commercial agreements, computer reservation systems (CRS), and ground handling. These block exemptions cover commercial agreements on the co-ordination of capacity, revenue pools, and consultations on fares and airport slot allocations. The CRS exemption gives free access to new airlines, elimination of bias, and the ability to cancel contracts without penalty, together with a code of conduct for the operation of Galileo and Amadeus. In the 1988 *Report on Competition Policy* the Commission states that it 'concurs with the view that block exemptions should not be "hewn in stone". It is for this reason that the regulations involved are required to contain clauses limiting the duration of their applicability.' In the 1987 *Report on Competition Policy* the Commission states that it grants block exemptions 'subject to strict conditions whose main purpose is to ensure that competition is neither eliminated nor unduly restricted as a result of the agreements and practices in question.'

Article 85.3 exemptions under the Treaty of Rome require that all four of the following conditions be met:
(1) there must be tangible benefits for production, distribution, or technical or economic progress;
(2) a fair share of such benefits must accrue to consumers;
(3) only restrictions on competition that are indispensable to achieving the beneficial results are allowed; and
(4) no substantial elimination of competition must occur.

In the light of the success of Anglo-Irish airline deregulation in increasing the output, profitability and productivity of the airlines it is difficult to argue that the consumers gain from preventing such developments throughout the EC. Substantial eliminations of competition occur where there is fare fixing, hub airport dominance, and ground handling monopoly.

DEVELOPMENTS ON IRELAND–CONTINENT ROUTES
The growth of traffic and reduction in fares on routes between Ireland and continental Europe have been less dramatic than

between Ireland and Britain. The proportion of passengers on Continental routes to Ireland–Britain routes fell from 48 per cent in 1985 to 34 per cent in 1989. While traffic on the Continental routes has grown by 63 per cent, traffic on the British routes has grown by 127 per cent.

In contrast to the substantial reductions in the unrestricted fare to London, no reduction took place in the fares from Dublin to the other EC capital cities between 1986 and 1988 for those on unrestricted tickets (table 8). The report on the first year of implementation of the December 1987 policy (EC, 1989, p. 5)

Table 8	**Development of fares, 1987–89, from Dublin (June 1987 = 100)**				
	ECONOMY FARES		EXCURSION FARES		EXCURSION/ ECONOMY (%)
	1988	1989	1988	1989	
Dublin to—					
Brussels	103.0	106.0	85.9	75.5	32.8
Copenhagen	103.2	106.1	97.6	100.4	43.1
Paris	103.1	106.3	68.0	54.4	27.9
Frankfurt	102.8	106.1	63.3	63.3	38.3
Rome	100	103.1	102.9	106.3	30.0
Amsterdam	103.2	106.4	64.2	54.1	33.4
Lisbon	100	100	103.2	70.7	25.7
London	56.7	51.9	111.6	91.3	29.4
Madrid	100	90	103.1	94.2	57.9
Inflation	102.1	105.0			

Note: The final column gives the excursion fare as a percentage of the economy fare in June 1989.

Source: EC (1989), annex B1.

found that 'generally the level of the Y fare has increased modestly, following more or less the rate of inflation.' It also found that the lowest published excursion fares in most cases increased slightly in 1988, and that in 1989 the proportion of excursion fares that were below 45 per cent of the economy fare was 60 per cent. In the case of 36 per cent of routes the lowest discount fare was below 40 per cent of the economy fare.

The excursion fares from Dublin to the cities shown in table 8 as a proportion of the economy fares are shown in the final column. These generally declined as a proportion of the economy fare between June 1987 and June 1989; for example the Dublin–Paris fare declined from 54.5 to 27.9 per cent of the economy fare. Only on the London route did the economy fare fall. The excursion fare also fell as a proportion of the economy fare, from 33.2 to 29.4 per cent.

In the summer of 1989 the Dublin–London fare was less than half of the fare on Continental routes shorter than 800 km (table 9). This contrasts with the situation in Europe as a whole, where fares per kilometre decline on longer journeys. For example in 1985 the ICAO fare survey found that the average fare on a 500 km journey was 30 per cent greater per passenger-kilometre than on a journey of 1,000 km. In Europe as a whole, fares per passenger-kilometre on a 500 km journey are 68 per cent greater than on a 2,000 km journey. By contrast, the Dublin–Rome and Dublin–Lisbon fares per kilometre are 55 per cent and 39 per cent greater, respectively, than on Dublin–London, which is only a quarter of the distance. The high-economy normal fares from Dublin to continental Europe are obviously out of line with those charged on Dublin–London since deregulation.

The discounted fares on the Continental routes are a larger proportion of the economy fare than on Dublin–London in the case of six of the eight Continental routes in table 8. The exceptions are Paris, which has the highest economy fare of all the routes in the table, and Lisbon, where the economy fare is 39 per cent greater, despite Lisbon's distance advantage over the much shorter London route. The excursion passenger on Dublin–London pays 29.4 per cent on average of an economy fare of 12.5p per kilometre, i.e. 3.7p per kilometre. The excursion passenger on Dublin–Paris pays 27.9 per cent of an economy fare of 30.1p per kilometre, i.e. 8.4p. Per kilometre, the Dublin–London excursion passenger pays 43.7 per cent of the excursion

	Comparative economy fares Dublin to London and continental European cities, summer 1989		
Table 9			
Dublin to—	FARE, ONE WAY	DISTANCE (KM)	COST PER KM
London	£58	463	12.5p
Amsterdam	£199	752	26.4p
Brussels	£212	784	27.0p
Frankfurt	£227	1088	20.9p
Paris	£238	790	30.1p
Copenhagen	£297	1241	23.9p
Madrid	£305	1456	20.9p
Lisbon	£342	1970	17.3p
Rome	£367	1896	19.3p

Source: *World Airline ABC*

fare to Paris; the Dublin–London economy passenger pays 41.4 per cent of the Dublin–Paris fare.

The fare reductions on the Continental routes have been confined to excursion fares. These still represent bad value compared with the excursion fares on Dublin–London. The Dublin–London economy fare has fallen by 48 per cent under deregulation, whereas no reduction has occurred in this fare to Continental destinations.

CAPACITY SHARING
The December 1987 agreement relaxed capacity sharing from the traditional 50/50 arrangement, reducing the guaranteed market share of the smaller party to the bilateral agreement to 40 per cent after 1988.

In Ireland this development had already taken place. British Airways chose in the past not to take up a 50 per cent share of Ireland–Britain air travel. Ireland has provided the bulk of the capacity on routes where the other country has shown less interest in the market. The EC reported that 'Ireland had special arrangements with the Netherlands and Italy because its airline operated partly on a country-pair monopoly basis.' In June 1989 Irish airlines provided 74.7 per cent of the capacity on air routes serving Ireland (table 10). Only Luxembourg had a higher proportion, with 77.5 per cent. In the case of all the other EC states the home country share in total aviation capacity ranged between 45 and 55 per cent. The Irish airlines' high share of the Irish market indicates that competition from outside Ireland is weak in the market and that competition from within the country is therefore more important than it is in other EC states in ensuring contestability.

Table 10	Community-wide capacity shares for individual member-states		
	JUNE 1987	JUNE 1988	JUNE 1989
Belgium	47.6	45.8	48.5
Denmark	54.4	50.4	48.2
France	49.0	50.8	51.3
Germany	45.6	45.2	48.4
Greece	47.9	48.8	49.1
Ireland	70.6	77.1	74.7
Italy	47.8	46.2	45.5
Luxembourg	75.6	77.8	77.5
Netherlands	53.0	52.3	49.7
Portugal	52.2	50.3	51.8
Spain	52.8	49.1	48.9
United Kingdom	48.1	47.9	47.7

Source: EC (1989), table 4.

MULTIPLE DESIGNATION

The designation of more than one airline per state to serve a route is a crucial part of deregulation in Europe. Given the tradition of collusion among the established airlines, new entrants are important in generating the benefits of competition in European aviation. Between 1987 and 1989 the number of routes with more than one carrier per EC member-state increased from 22 to 33. The EC reported that only five member-states had given their airlines the benefit of multiple designation: these were Germany, Ireland, Italy, Netherlands, and United Kingdom.

THE CONTESTABILITY OF DEREGULATED AVIATION MARKETS

The theory of contestable markets has two important implications for public policy. Entry to the market must not be restricted; and there may be cases in industries with small numbers of producers where the contestability of the market can be improved by public policy (Baumol, 1982).

In a contestable market, efficiency is ensured by potential entrants who enter the market if the existing suppliers raise their prices above those that could be charged by the new entrants. The evidence from the United States is that actual market entry is more effective than potential market entry in ensuring efficiency. Deregulation in the United States has left important sources of economic rent for established airlines in place. Table 11 shows eight barriers to contestability in a deregulated airline industry. It is based on Levine (1987) and Bailey and Williams (1988), and also on the experience of deregulation between Ireland and Britain. Table 11 also shows policy response options; some of these policies would increase the contestability of the market. Policies to promote contestability in a deregulated market are recommended by Baumol (1982) and Pryke (1989). Pryke warns that 'if liberalisation is not to turn out a monopolistic damp squib it is vital that Governments and the EC should do everything possible to foster competition and make airline routes as contestable as possible.' Without a pro-contestability policy the established airlines will be able to use their sources of economic rent to deter new entrants and to finance price wars against actual entrants.

Baumol's policy prescription that 'in some cases the contestability of the market can be increased by public policy' has assumed new relevance as several analyses of the US aviation

21

Table 11	Barriers to contestability in a deregulated airline industry	

BARRIER	POLICY RESPONSE OPTIONS
Hub airport dominance	Ban new entrants
	Cap existing services
	Auction slots
	Slot lottery
	Administrative intervention
Predatory pricing	Application of article 86 of Treaty of Rome to aviation controls over geographical price discrimination or passenger discrimination
Ground handling monopolies	Competition in handling for reward
State aids	Transparency and equal eligibility for subsidies
CRS bias	Neutrality rules; divestiture
Price collusion	Application of article 85 of Treaty of Rome to aviation
Anti-competitive mergers	Control by EC competition policy directorate
Thin route monopoly	Competition for the market

industry since deregulation have found important barriers to contestability, albeit within a policy change that remains a substantial net benefit to the US economy as a whole (Levine, 1987; Bailey and Williams, 1988; Kahn, 1988; Pryke, 1989). There are now significant barriers to contestability in a deregulated aviation sector. If these prevent new entry, a major assumption underlying the theory of contestable markets is invalidated. Freed from the threat of new entrants, the industry may become again collusive and oligopolistic.

In the case of two barriers to contestability, the EC has adopted more contestable positions than the United States. These are seen in the response to the takeover by British Airways of British Caledonian, and to bias in computer reservations systems. The EC has powers under article 86 of the Treaty of Rome to deal with predatory pricing as an abuse of a dominant position, and under article 85 to deal with price fixing. Thus British Airways was required to divest itself of slots at Gatwick when it acquired British Caledonian. The EC also has a code of conduct to prevent abuse of dominant position by airlines that own computer reservation systems.

HUB AIRPORT DOMINANCE

The most important obstacle to contestability in a deregulated aviation sector is hub airport dominance. If new airlines are excluded from major airports, their ability to woo passengers from existing airlines will be limited. The established airlines can earn economic rents at the dominated hub; this rent can be used to fund predatory pricing elsewhere.

Hub airport dominance forces new entrants to develop at lesser airports, thereby losing the possibility of attracting interlining traffic at the busy hub. It is usually combined with the allocation of airport capacity, or slots, on a seniority or 'grandfather rights' basis. Outright bans on new entrants, as at Heathrow since 1977, are the most extreme form of 'grandfather rights'. All of the increase from 22 million to 38 million passengers since then was allocated to the existing airlines by administrative decision: an obvious violation of the contestability conditions. The ban on new entrants was not necessitated by capacity constraints. According to the CAA (1986), 'had the present rules not been introduced, the international scheduled services thus prevented could have been operated at Heathrow, although in some cases with great difficulty.'

Bailey and Williams (1988, p. 199) comment that 'airport authorities need to make airport access available on fair and reasonable terms that give all carriers an equal opportunity to compete and that conform to the rights of private citizens to enforce these duties. Antitrust authorities need to look at carriers' abilities to extract rents based on local monopoly positions at hub airports, not just at national monopoly characteristics.'

The criteria set out by Bailey and Williams are obviously not complied with by banning new entrants. Capping existing services was proposed by the CAA (1986) at four round trips per day per carrier at Heathrow.

The auction of airport slots, with ring fences around categories such as domestic, long-haul, short-haul, and charter, has been proposed by TWA and Pan Am. It has been opposed by the CAA, on the grounds that the competition in the slot auction would not be on a level playing field. The CAA (1985, 3.31) stated: 'Charter operators at Gatwick and domestic carriers at Heathrow engaged in a competitive market would be competing for slots against international carriers operating in an environment of limited frequency, monopolistic pricing practices and pooling agreements. It is open to question whether, in these circumstances, use of the price mechanism would produce an allocation of resources which could rationally be described as efficient.' Without the ring fences, large international carriers would acquire a large number of slots, to the detriment of other services. However, many slots are used inefficiently now by small aircraft.

A lottery to allocate slots would overcome the obstacles faced by smaller new airlines at slot auctions. 'Use it or lose it' conditions would have to be imposed to ensure the use of the slots. No revenue would accrue to the airport authority under this system of space allocation at airports. The auction system on the other hand would give airports an incentive not to invest in extra capacity where it might drive down the price of slots at the auction.

Administrative intervention to allocate airport space has included the removal of charter flights from busy airports, and the curtailment of all-cargo flights. The removal of small domestic services with low interline content was proposed by the CAA in the case of services from Heathrow to Dundee, Carlisle, Inverness, Guernsey, Plymouth, Isle of Man, and Jersey. Despite previous attempts to discourage general aviation at Heathrow and Gatwick, these airports had 31,000 such movements in 1984. If these were converted into passenger numbers at 100 passengers per plane, capacity could be increased by 3.1 million passengers.

The object of increasing the efficiency of each slot on congested urban roads, either in road pricing or bus lanes—the administrative counterpart—is to increase the efficiency of the system by more intensive use of vehicles, and rewarding the bus, which is an efficient user of scarce urban road space. The efficiency of airport slots could also be improved. For example, a 4 per cent increase in the number of passengers per air transport movement would increase the capacity of Heathrow from 38 million to 56 million passengers within a decade.

At present, airport capacity at congested airports is allocated by scheduling committees of airline representatives. The activities of these committees enjoy exemption under article 85.3 of the Treaty of Rome from the provisions against price collusion and market sharing, despite the obvious anti-competitive aspects of their work.

Hub airport dominance is a function both of the different sizes of airlines and the failure of governments to deal with the obstacles to the expansion of airport and air traffic control capacity. It is not surprising that these policies, combined with the failure to price these scarce facilities at their marginal opportunity costs, have reduced contestability. If underinvestment in the infrastructure is to remain a feature of much of European and US aviation, other means of allocating infrastructure to new airlines will be required in order to increase the contestability of the aviation sector.

Allied to hub airport dominance as an obstacle to contestability is the problem of price predation. Potential entry is not sufficient to deter overcharging. To quote Kahn, 'market concentration does matter and the general trend over time has been toward the conclusion that it matters a great deal.'

PREDATORY PRICING

The problem of predation is exacerbated by failure to invest in airport capacity, coupled with the allocation of existing slots to established airlines. It is likely to persist, however, unless there is a referee in contests between airlines of different sizes. Kahn finds here that the assumptions of contestability break down. 'I take perverse satisfaction in having predicted the demise of price-cutting competitors like World and Capital Airways if we did nothing to limit the predictable geographically discriminatory response to the incumbent carriers to their entry, and in having rejected the conventional wisdom that predation would not pay because any attempt to raise fares after the departure of the price-cutting newcomers would elicit instantaneous competitive reentry.' In dealing with problems of predation on certain airline routes, the EC has powers under article 86 of the Treaty of Rome to prevent abuse of a dominant position. Cases of geographical price discrimination would have to be justified by reference to cost differences specific to each route examined. The differences in fares charged to different passengers could also be examined in relation to the cost of each passenger category. If an airline is able to implement a fare reduction on some routes but not on others, the onus is on the market regulator to investigate why this disparity of performance exists.

Much of the present structure of pricing by airlines in Europe does not reflect cost differences in the type of product supplied. Peak load pricing could be used to reflect the higher cost of serving the peak, while lower fares would be charged at off-peak times and days. The pricing actually used by European airlines includes discounts for advance bookings, although airlines do not normally change aircraft types or frequencies over the booking period. It also includes discounts for those who stay away over Saturday night; but these also fail to take into account the cost to the airline of the actual return journey time chosen.

GROUND HANDLING MONOPOLIES

Competition in ground handling is not normal in European aviation. The service choice facing a new airline may be to use the national airline of the state in which the airport is located, or to provide the service itself. It is not usual to have a full range of competitive choice, and it is expensive for a new entrant to have to provide the service itself.

British Midland is the second-largest carrier at Heathrow in terms of aircraft movements. It was compelled to use an airline with grandfather rights in handling at Heathrow or to use its major competitor, British Airways. The issue was examined by the Monopolies and Mergers Commission (1985, p. 41), which recommended that in deciding ground handling arrangements the British Airports Authority should 'not limit its consideration to airlines with existing self-handling rights and should take account of the charges made to airlines and the cost savings available.'

The Monopolies and Mergers Commission did not recommend the deregulation of ground handling, because there might be congestion caused by an excessive number of ground handling vehicles. Restricting the number of vehicles could be done through the price mechanism. Restricting the number of producers merely increases the monopolistic rents of the handling operators at the expense of airlines without handling rights. A free market in ground handling is recommended in table 11. There is no economic reason why the activity cannot be deregulated.

STATE AIDS TO AVIATION
Governments frequently aid airlines by underwriting losses, by loan guarantees, and by so-called equity capital injections. Competition is thus distorted where other airlines do not receive these aids or receive smaller subsidies. Where governments decide to intervene in aviation markets, for example by requiring airlines to perform 'social services' on thin routes, there should be competitive tendering for such services, so that the least-cost airline with the lowest subsidy provides the service. Subsidies should be transparent, and all airlines in a market should have equal eligibility for the subsidies available.

BIAS IN COMPUTER RESERVATION SYSTEMS
In the United States, control of the computer reservation systems (CRS) has been a major source of profit for airlines. Access to these systems is essential if new airlines wish to sell through travel agents.

There are two main sources of bias against new airlines in the operation of CRS by established airlines. Since 90 per cent of bookings are made from the first display, a programme to show new airlines only on subsequent displays would place them at a disadvantage. The charging of high fees to new airlines for the use of CRS would both place the new airlines at a cost disadvantage and increase the revenues of the established airlines that owned the CRS. Ownership of CRS also provides the established airline with valuable commercial information on the yields and traffic flows of the new entrants. CRS also yields large profits.

The EC has devised neutrality rules for the operation of CRS in Europe. The EC fined Sabena 100,000 ECU for refusing London European Airways access to its CRS, Saphire. The Galileo and Amadeus systems are both owned by a group of airlines, so that no one airline can gain control. In the United States, on the other hand, large airlines controlled the CRS, such as American's

Sabre, United's Apollo, and TWA-Northwest's Pars. If it is not possible to devise a neutral operation for Europe's CRS, then divestiture could be considered. It would then be illegal to own both an airline and a CRS, and there would be an arm's-length relationship between the aviation and CRS industries.

PRICE COLLUSION
Price collusion has been a long-established feature of international aviation in Europe. Traditionally, governments readily accepted the fares submitted jointly by national airlines and agreed between airlines through the International Air Transport Association (IATA) fare-fixing machinery.

Price fixing by airlines enjoys an exemption until 31 January 1991 under article 85.3 of the Treaty of Rome. There is no economic reason why it should continue to do so. The EC Commission has the power to impose fines of up to 10 per cent of annual turnover for price fixing and forming cartels: fines of 57.85 million ECU were imposed on fifteen members of a polypropylene cartel in 1986 (EC, *Report on Competition Policy*, 1986, p. 57).

ANTI-COMPETITIVE MERGERS
In the takeover by British Airways of British Caledonian, the EC Commission reduced the potential anti-competitive aspect by requiring British Airways to divest itself of certain slots at Gatwick. This prevented it from establishing hub airport dominance at Gatwick as well as at Heathrow.

A number of European takeovers are in progress in 1990. These include a proposal for British Airways and SAS to each take a 20 per cent stake in Sabena; an Air France takeover of both Air Inter and UTA; and a KLM proposal to take a 40 per cent stake in Transavia. SAS, Lufthansa, Air France, KLM and Swissair have taken stakes in small airlines that might have been competitors in time. The French government in 1989 refused UTA many route applications and favoured Air France for the routes.

The evidence therefore is that without a pro-contestability policy by the EC and member-states, the airline industry will become increasingly oligopolistic and many of the gains from deregulation will be lost in the deregulated markets and may never be achieved in markets such as Germany, Scandinavia, France, and Italy.

THE THIN ROUTE MONOPOLY PROBLEM

Where a route can only sustain a single airline there may be scope for charging more than on routes where actual competition exists. Regulation of prices charged would involve comparison with fares on contested routes, with the requirement that the thin route monopoly airline explain the difference. A further possible approach is to have competition *for* the market where it is not possible *in* the market, as recommended by Demsetz.

A PRO-CONTESTABILITY POLICY IN EUROPEAN AVIATION

Table 11 sets the agenda for a pro-contestability policy in European aviation. The expiry of the airlines' block exemptions from competition policy in January 1991 leaves little time to complete the internal market by 1 January 1993. The block exemptions, combined with the lack of a policy on predatory pricing, place at risk the gains from the entry of new airlines that have been seen in the examples of deregulation and liberalisation in Europe. The ability of larger, higher-cost airlines to kill off new entrants has been an unwelcome feature of US airline deregulation. In Europe a tradition of high-cost national airlines means that the gains from fully contestable markets are potentially large. On the other hand the tradition of price collusion between state airlines and the regulatory capture by state airlines of governments, allied with minimal application of competition policy to aviation, makes investment in new-entrant airlines an unattractive proposition. The full gains from deregulation for the economy as a whole require new market entrants; but the absence of a competition policy in the sector will deter investors and the new airlines.

In October 1990 the EC agreed to Air France's takeover of UTA, giving Air France a 97 per cent share of French aviation. Air France lost its monopoly of ten domestic and fifty international routes, but was required to sell its 35 per cent stake in TAT, the fourth-largest French airline, by the middle of 1992. The takeover makes Air France by far the largest airline in the EC, with 32.6 million passengers in 1989, compared with 23.2 million for British Airways. The takeover removes two independent potential competitors in a contestable EC market.

The promotion of a contestable market in European aviation is vital to an island economy such as Ireland's. This issue is examined again in chapter 6.

AIRPORTS AND AIRLINE COMPETITION

Airports are important in promoting competition between airlines. We have already examined the difficulties facing new airlines because of the control of airports by established airlines. Airports are also a significant cost to airlines (table 12). There is also evidence that failure to invest adequately in airports and related infrastructure may prevent the growth of aviation.

Pricing in European aviation was based in the past on cost recovery. In a price-competitive environment there will be pressure for cost reductions in areas such as handling and navigation charges. Competition in handling has already been proposed; competitive tendering for the provision of air traffic control has reduced these costs in many British airports (Barrett, 1984 and 1987).

The EC (1984) estimated that airport and air-space user charges accounted for 25.9 per cent of scheduled airline costs within the EC. The composition of these costs is shown in table 12.

Table 12	**Airport and air-space charges as a proportion of airline costs**	
Aircraft and passenger handling		12.22%
Aircraft passenger charges		5.15%
Landing charges		4.07%
En-route navigation		3.61%
Airport navigation		0.85%
		25.90%
Source: EC (1984), p.25.		

AIRPORT INVESTMENT

Since airport investment in Ireland has anticipated demand, the 'grandfather rights' system is not used to allocate airport space. Many European countries have failed to invest ahead of projected airport demand: the Association of European Airlines estimates that nineteen major European airports will face congestion by 1995. There is also serious underinvestment in air traffic control.

The obstacles to expansion of investment in European aviation infrastructure are environmental and political rather than economic. Increased traffic by air generates revenues for the providers of airports and other infrastructure. Airlines pay for this infrastructure. While Irish airport investment has been ahead of demand, the lack of investment in airport infrastructure elsewhere in Europe limits the expansion of Irish aviation. The lack of capacity at Heathrow and Gatwick is reinforced by the commitment to ban night flying and to curtail investment.

ENVIRONMENTAL OBJECTIONS TO EXPANSION OF LONDON AIRPORTS

The following quotations from the British government paper *Airports Policy* indicate the public policy reasons for restricting the growth of Heathrow and Gatwick. 'The Government has stated on several occasions in the past that it did not intend to provide a fifth terminal at the airport. Its conclusion was based on a number of factors, including the noise climate and disturbance to people living around Heathrow; the difficulty of removing the Parry Oaks sludge disposal facilities to make way for the terminal; the generally restricted site at the airport; the problem of providing adequate surface access and the ability of runways to handle the additional traffic.'

At Gatwick 'the Government believes that the provision of a second runway would have unacceptable environmental implications. It could only be built to the north of the present runway, which would require a major expansion of the airport's boundaries and bring the runway within a mile of the built-up area around Horley. The village of Charlwood would be destroyed and other nearby villages would be seriously affected. Furthermore, it is by no means certain that the capacity of a two-runway airport could be fully utilised because of air traffic control constraints arising from the proximity of Heathrow and defence establishments.'

AIRPORTS AND THE ENVIRONMENT

In matters such as bans on night flying and the expansion of runway capacity at Gatwick and Stansted, environmental lobbies have exercised a veto over expansion. Coase shows the superiority in economic efficiency of negotiable property rights over a veto. In analysing the social costs and benefits of airport development, the following factors should be included:

(1) *The measures of noise nuisance from airports have fallen.* The report *Airports Policy* estimated that 'the area within the 35 NNI [noise and nuisance index] fell from 826 sq. kms to 507 sq. kms between 1974 and 1983.' ICAO chapter 3 noise standards will further reduce noise levels at airports.

(2) *Some noise nuisance compensation has already been paid.* Noise insulation grants have been approved for 41,000 dwellings near Heathrow and Gatwick.

(3) *Noise nuisance costs have been capitalised.* The majority of properties near Heathrow were built after construction of the airport began in 1944. Properties purchased since then have included in their price both the noise nuisance disamenity and an enhancement factor caused by the economic activity generated by the airport. The evidence is that the economic activity generated by airports enhances property values more than the noise nuisance reduces them. Compensation should be paid only to those who suffer a drop in property values following an airport investment announcement. Owners of blighted properties should have the right to sell to the airport company; the airport company is likely to gain subsequently when property values rise. The success of environmental groups in opposing airports has, through the 'grandfather rights' system, created substantial economic rents for the dominant airlines and airport managers at the airports concerned.

AIRPORT REVENUES

The receipts of Aer Rianta are divided almost evenly between operational and commercial activity. The former comprises aircraft landing fees, passenger load fees, and rents and concessions. The commercial revenue comprises shopping, catering, tours and banquets, and mail order. Table 13 shows the revenues for 1989.

DUTY-FREE SHOPS

Aer Rianta derived 36 per cent of its revenue from shopping receipts in 1989. The duty-free concession to international

Table 13	Aer Rianta revenue, 1989	
OPERATIONAL	**£ MILLION**	
Aircraft landing and parking fees	17.7	
Passenger load fees	21.4	
Rents and concessions	19.3	
Other	0.4	
Total operational	58.9	
COMMERCIAL		
Shopping and mail order	45.2	
Catering	8.7	
Banquets	2.0	
Rianta International	7.6	
Other	1.9	
Total commercial	65.6	
Total revenue	124.5	

transport by Ministers for Finance allows airlines, shipping companies and airports to sell certain products without charging sales taxes. The concession is highly lucrative.

Ireland in 1985 had the highest excise duties in the EC, at 7.63 per cent of GDP compared with the UK at 4.35 per cent, and the Netherlands, the lowest, at 1.92 per cent.

The International Duty-Free Confederation in 1989 submitted to the EC that 'for Irish airports the decision to abolish duty free travel (DFT) allowances will put ECU 15 mn [£11.6 million] of profits at risk, assuming that the equivalent of half of the inter-EC profit of DFT sales of perfumes, gifts and other products will be recovered through retail activities. If recovery is made only from inter-EC traffic fees for inter-EC passengers may rise by 39 per cent.'

The EIU report estimates that the value of duty-free sales in Europe in 1987 was $4,641.2 million. Half the sales occurred at airport shops (36 per cent) or airlines (14 per cent), while 'other', comprising military, diplomatic and other sales, accounted for 29 per cent. The composition of the revenue was: liquor 32.7 per cent, fragrances 25.3 per cent, tobacco 23.1 per cent, and 'other' 18.9 per cent.

The Aer Rianta annual report for 1988 stated that 'we will be arguing very strongly that the elimination of duty free sales would have an adverse effect on travel costs, tourism and commerce and would place the European Community at a disadvantage vis-a-vis surrounding countries.'

The duty-free concession is obviously valuable to airports. The development of other forms of retailing for the large captive market at airports is unlikely to yield the same high margins as duty-free. On the other hand the harmonisation of indirect taxes within the EC will diminish the attractiveness of duty-free shops in high-duty countries such as Ireland. The duty-free concession is difficult to defend in the context of Ireland's fiscal problems. Aviation in the US internal market has developed without the subsidy of duty-free sales, whereas in Europe, notwithstanding this subsidy, a high-cost aviation system has developed. Since the goal of the internal market is to promote efficiency, it is difficult to defend the retention of the duty-free subsidy.

IRISH REGIONAL AIRPORTS AND ANGLO-IRISH LIBERALISATION

The liberalisation of Anglo-Irish aviation in 1986 has had a very strong impact on the Irish regional airports.

The analysis of Ireland–Britain traffic by airport shows a decline in the years 1980–85 and a steep increase in 1986 and subsequent years. The decline occurred at Dublin, with Cork and Shannon either stationary or rising slightly. No new airport had been opened for international scheduled service since Cork Airport in 1961. Cork had a persistent record of losses over the period.

Since 1986, international service has been provided at Knock, Waterford, Galway, Kerry, Sligo, and Donegal. By 1989 these airports had 280,000 passengers on UK services, or 7 per cent of the total market. The success of the new airports when compared

Table 14	Air travel between Ireland and Britain by Irish airport, 1980–89 (000)			
	1980	1985	1989	INDEX 1980 = 100
Dublin	1,523	1,482	3,167	208
Cork	212	212	385	182
Shannon	151	158	322	213
Knock	—	—	170	
Waterford	—	—	50	
Galway	—	—	35	
Kerry	—	—	25 *	
	1,886	1,852	4,200	223
All regional airports†				
	363	370	987	267

* Opened May 1989.
† Cork, Shannon and new airports

with the stagnation of the older regional airports under pre-deregulation policies is remarkable. The new airports in 1989 had 77 per cent more passengers on British routes than Shannon in 1985, and 32 per cent more than Cork. The impact of deregulation on the regional airports has been dramatic. Cork, Shannon and the new airports have increased their passenger numbers on British routes from 270,000 in 1986 to 987,000 in 1989, an increase of 167 per cent. This compares with 108 per cent out of Dublin.

AIRPORTS AND REGIONAL DEVELOPMENT
Deregulation of aviation between Ireland and Britain has brought unprecedented and largely unforeseen growth in the regional airports, in particular at the new airports. The success of Anglo-Irish deregulation in promoting the development of regional airports in Ireland contrasts with the lack of development

arising from the EC Regional Air Services Directive of 1984. Because of pressure from established airlines, the EC regional services were limited to seventy seats, banned from category 1 airports, and restricted in both direct and indirect competition with established services.

The success of regional airports in Ireland under deregulation removed an argument made for regulation. That case was that part of the £208 Dublin–London fare cross-subsidised remote or unprofitable routes. Since deregulation, fares on the main routes have fallen, and services to the regions have expanded to more airports than were served under regulation. In addition the fares to the new airports have been lower than those charged from the established regional airports. For example, in the summer of 1989 the Galway–London fare was £148 on a new route, or 60 per cent of the £240 fare charged on Shannon–London.

THE GAINS FROM REGIONAL AIRPORTS

The gains to the Irish regions from the establishment of the new airports have been significant. The airport at Knock was controversial because of its high construction costs, but has generated significant time savings for an annual traffic of 170,000 on British routes and about 10,000 domestic passengers. It is the largest of the new airports, as table 14 shows.

Before the opening of Knock airport a journey from that part of Co. Mayo to a London airport took about five-and-a-half hours. This comprised four hours' driving time, with the prospect of congestion at Mullingar and between Maynooth and Dublin and between the city and the airport; twenty minutes' check-in time; and a seventy-minute flight. Since the opening of Knock the journey time is eighty minutes, with twenty minutes' check-in time: a reduction in overall journey time of 70 per cent.

An in-flight survey on Ryanair routes in December 1988 found an average income per passenger of £15,250. This is the equivalent of £7.33 per hour, or £27.10 for the time saving of 3 hours 50 minutes on the London journey. For the 170,000 passengers who flew to Britain from Knock in 1989 the value of time saved was £4.6 million.

The units of time saved per passenger on the other new routes may be smaller. For instance, Galway passengers might have used Shannon in the absence of their local airport, Kerry passengers might have chosen Cork, and Waterford passengers might have chosen Dublin. An average time saving of two hours for these 110,000 passengers would generate annual time savings of £1.6 million. The combined value of time savings generated by all the regional airports with international service is therefore £6.2 million, based on 1989 traffic volumes.

In addition to the development of direct international service, the regional airports have since 1986 developed feeder services to Dublin with access to the Aer Lingus network. The number of domestic air passengers increased from 300,000 in 1985 to 669,000 in 1989. This includes the Dublin–Shannon leg of travel from Dublin to North America. The number of trans-atlantic passengers at Dublin increased from 169,000 in 1985 to 273,000 in 1989. The remaining regional traffic therefore increased from 131,000 in 1985 to 396,000 in 1989.

REALLOCATING AIR-SPACE PROPERTY RIGHTS
Large parts of European air-space are reserved for military use. The administrative division of air-space between civilian and military use was made when civil aviation was on a far smaller scale than today. In France it is estimated that military aircraft account for 10 per cent of total air traffic, yet 40 per cent of the air-space is reserved for military use. On Brussels–Zürich the average civil aircraft has to travel a route 45 per cent longer than the direct route. There is an average extra journey length of 10 per cent in Europe because of military zones.

The opportunity cost of military use of air-space should be made explicit in defence budgets. The creation of a market in air-space will provide the data for the use of satellites at high level for surveillance work and the transfer of military training to air-space with low civilian demand as alternatives. Demsetz points out that the appropriateness of recognising a property right depends on the scarcity of the resource relative to the cost of enforcing the property right. When land was abundant it was treated as common property. Air-space is now scarce, and a system of property rights is appropriate.

AIR FREIGHT
Air freight in 1989 accounted for 15.5 per cent of Irish foreign trade by value and 0.2 per cent by volume. Table 15 shows the

growth of air freight at the three state airports. While volumes grew by 20 per cent between 1970 and 1975, growth was only 6.6 per cent between 1975 and 1989. By contrast, passenger numbers increased by 14 per cent between 1970 and 1975 and by 106 per cent between 1975 and 1989. Air freight is therefore of declining relative importance in the development of Irish airports. The overall development of Irish overseas freight movements will be examined in the chapter on ports and shipping.

Table 15	**Air freight handled at major Irish airports (tonnes)**			
	Cork	Dublin	Shannon	Total
1970	1,340	39,805	9,702	50,847
1975	3,436	44,731	17,397	65,564
1980	1,078	43,347	16,604	60,029
1985	1,523	41,956	25,027	68,506
1989	2,057	46,932	21,363	70,352

Source: Aer Rianta annual accounts.

PORTS AND SHIPPING

Ports handled 64 per cent of the value of Irish foreign trade in 1989: this compares with 15.5 per cent for airports and 19 per cent for the land frontier with Northern Ireland. Ports account for 80 per cent of the volume of Irish foreign trade, compared with 20 per cent using the land frontier; the airports' share is only 0.2 per cent.

Table 16 shows the changes in foreign trade by ports between 1964 and 1989. Seaports declined from 80.6 per cent of the value of foreign trade to 64.2 per cent; the airports' and land frontier's shares both increased. Within the seaports sector, Dublin and Cork showed relative declines, while Rosslare and Dún Laoghaire increased.

2

Table 16			
Share of Irish foreign trade by value, 1964–89			
		1964 (%)	1989 (%)
Seaports		80.6	64.2
—of which	Dublin	55.2	32.5
	Cork	12.0	5.2
	Waterford	4.9	6.2
	Rosslare	1.0	10.4
	Dún Laoghaire	*nil*	6.5
	Others	7.5	4.6
Land frontier		11.3	19.1
Airports		8.1	15.5

Source: Central Statistics Office.

The tonnage of goods handled at seaports increased by 36 per cent between 1980 and 1989. The series 'Statistics of Port

Table 17	Market shares of volume of goods handled by ports, 1989 (%)
Dublin	24.5
Limerick	22.5
Cork	22.4
Waterford	4.8
Drogheda	4.4
Foynes	4.1
New Ross	4.0
Rosslare	2.6
Greenore	2.0
Galway	1.6
Dundalk	1.4
Dún Laoghaire	1.2
Arklow	1.1
Wicklow	0.9
Sligo	0.2
Others	2.7
	100

Traffic' shows the breakdown by port of the 1989 tonnage, as shown in table 17.

A comparison of the market shares by value of traffic from table 16 and by volume of traffic from table 17 shows that Dún Laoghaire, Rosslare, Dublin and Waterford have higher market shares of traffic by value of goods shipped than by volume. Cork, Limerick, Drogheda, New Ross and Foynes have higher shares by volume than by value.

Table 18 shows the changes in output of seaports by type of traffic between 1980 and 1989. The growth of lift-on/lift-off (LOLO) traffic was greater than the growth of the total market, while the market share of roll-on/roll-off (RORO) traffic declined. The average size of ship increased by 42 per cent. The number

Changes in activity at Irish ports, 1980-89

	1980	1989	INDEX
Number of arrivals	13,507	12,928	96
Net register tonnage (000)	19,370	25,940	134
Total goods handled (000 tonnes)	18,357	24,896	136
RORO (000 tonnes)	1,807	2,344	130
LOLO (000 tonnes)	1,802	3,099	172
All other traffic (000 tonnes)	14,748	19,453	132

Source: Central Statistics Office, Statistics of Port Traffic in 1989.

of ship arrivals declined by 4 per cent, but the net register tonnage increased by 34 per cent.

The RORO traffic market shares in 1989 were: Dublin, 57 per cent; Rosslare, 28 per cent; Dún Laoghaire, 13 per cent; and Cork, under 2 per cent. The LOLO market shares in 1988 were: Dublin, 56 per cent; Waterford, 33 per cent; and Cork, 11 per cent.

IRISH PORTS POLICY

The 1985 Green Paper on transport policy stated that 'the basic philosophy underlying Irish ports policy has been that ports should, in principle, be operated as commercial undertakings and be financially self-supporting.' Harbour grants 'should be provided only where improvements are essential to meet well defined commercial needs, and where a harbour authority's own resources are insufficient.'

As examples of grant assistance where there was no strong evidence of a 'well defined commercial need' the Green Paper cites the developments at Ringaskiddy, Co. Cork, where harbour dredging, a car ferry terminal and deep-water wharf cost £30 million, and dredging at Sligo, on which £0.7 million was spent in the hope of attracting new traffic. When Dublin Port got into difficulties in the middle 1980s the Government gave grant assistance of £3 million a year for 1985, 1986, and 1987, and guaranteed loans of £7 million. The Green Paper noted that 'an analysis of ports' profitability for the five year period to 1983 carried out by the Department of Communications showed that, while all but three of the top fourteen scheduled harbours were profitable, the surpluses generated tended to be quite small. The return on capital averaged only 2 per cent.'

The 1988 Comprehensive Public Expenditure Programme stated that 'for commercial harbours the objective is that harbour authorities should operate on a commercial basis and be self-supporting.' The fourteen scheduled ports run by harbour boards had revenues of £30.2 million in 1988.

The National Development Plan, 1989–93, projected the expenditure of £72 million on port development at Dublin, Rosslare, Waterford, and Cork, with external funding from the European Regional Development Fund (ERDF). This compares with capital expenditures of £6.7 million in 1987 and £8.2 million in 1988, financed by the Local Loans Fund and the harbour boards' own resources. On completion of this investment the financing of port investment should be based on commercial borrowing and on revenue guarantees and advances from users.

THE MANAGEMENT OF IRISH PORTS

The cumbersome local-authority type of administration of Irish ports has been criticised in recent years. In 1984 a review of Dublin Port was conducted by the Labour Court. The report of the Dublin Docks Review Group points out the difficulties of operating ports with a local-authority type of management board. 'A Board of 23 members, none of whom is paid and many of whom will naturally see themselves as representatives of special interests, could hardly be expected to provide the strong, competent and united leadership which the development of Dublin Port requires.' The Review Group recommended the replacement of the Port and Docks Board with a state company. The Dublin Chamber of Commerce 'would welcome a thorough review of the port, its debt structure, labour policies, plant utilisation and, indeed, its possible restructuring into a smaller, more commercial format, freed from the constraints of having to accommodate the vested interests of many diverse groups on its board. The Chamber takes the view that the port board's status—which is similar to that of a local authority—is inappropriate to its competitive function.'

In addition to the state company favoured by the Labour Court, the privatisation of ports is a policy option. The privatisation of the associated ports in Britain in 1981 and 1984 transferred nineteen docks from public to private ownership. These included Southampton, Hull, and Cardiff. The market capitalisation of the company has steadily increased.

USE OF NORTHERN IRELAND PORTS

Between 1964 and 1989 the share of Irish foreign trade by value using the land frontier with Northern Ireland increased from 11.3 to 19.1 per cent. In 1989, £5,185 million of Irish foreign trade passed over the border. Only £1,222 million, or 25 per cent, was Northern Ireland trade; the other origins and destinations were: Britain, 56 per cent; other Europe, 16 per cent; and rest of world, 3 per cent.

The Dublin Chamber of Commerce estimated in February 1990 that 'almost 40 per cent of RoRo loads between the Republic and London travels via Northern Ireland, despite the extra 300 miles of road travel involved.' The report found a 'huge discrepancy in ferry rates on a mileage or time basis' between Larne and Stranraer and between Dún Laoghaire and Holyhead, and lower port costs, cheaper customs clearance costs at the land frontier and lower road haulage costs for Northern Ireland carriers. The report states that the cost and service factors that have diverted business to Larne 'represent the challenge to the Central Corridor which is simply not doing its job.' The loss from the diversion of traffic through Northern Ireland was estimated at £56 million per year. Total trade transiting through Northern Ireland in 1988 was 2.2 million tonnes, of which 33 per cent was 'natural' Northern Ireland traffic. The loss of Republic of Ireland traffic was therefore 1.5 million tonnes per year, according to the Chamber.

PORTS POLICY IN THE 1990s

The loss of port traffic to Northern Ireland ports is being tackled by an EC-backed investment plan. Management efficiency in the Republic's ports will also have to be improved, and the efficiency of road hauliers and shipping companies made competitive with those at present available to and from Northern Ireland ports.

COMPETITION AND PORTS

Fifteen ports within the Republic compete actively for its foreign trade. In addition Northern Ireland ports, such as Larne, Belfast, and Warrenpoint, seek the trade, and there are a number of other ports currently doing little business but available to re-enter the market.

The 1985 Green Paper stated that 'the Minister believes that a single authority is necessary for the future exploitation of the Shannon estuary and that it would lead to a more efficient use of resources.' The case for other amalgamations of ports was made as follows (6.20): 'Rationalisation of the structure of other harbour authorities to prevent unnecessary competition for scarce Exchequer funds is also desirable. The overall concern must be to ensure that there is sufficient and adequate portal facilities nationally and for each of the regions. However, local bodies sometimes cloud commercial judgement and rivalry between neighbouring ports sometimes acts as the main spur to unneces-sary and costly port development. There is a need for more co-operation between adjoining ports. Consideration is therefore being given to the benefits of grouping together certain harbour authorities such as, for example, Dundalk and Drogheda, Arklow and Wicklow, Waterford and New Ross, and Cork and Kinsale.' The Green Paper also proposed 'transfer of responsibility to the new Dublin Port Authority' as an option for Dún Laoghaire.

The movements in market shares indicate that, in the opera-tion of ports, economies of scale are not important. Several large ports have lost market share over the period since 1964. While the Green Paper is concerned about overinvestment at new ports, the costs of servicing the investment, combined with port operating costs, have not deterred the growth of market share at ports other than the traditional major ports. On the other hand the creation of local monopolies, as proposed in the Green Paper, would remove the incentive to control operating costs that competition promotes. Drogheda, Wicklow, Dún Laoghaire, New Ross and Kinsale are therefore constraining influences on the growth of costs at Dundalk, Arklow, Dublin, Waterford, and Cork, respectively. To prevent port competition by amalgamating adjoining ports, as suggested in the Green Paper, would reduce the efficiency of the ports.

Competition in the ports sector also requires free access to ports. While the legal ownership of airports is not held by airlines, in practice the capacity at airports is controlled by the established airlines through the 'grandfather rights' system. In ports there must also be a system of efficiently allocating capacity between established and new shipping companies.

STATE POLICY AND SHIPPING COMPANIES

Irish Shipping Ltd was set up to meet the nation's strategic shipping needs during the 1939–45 war. Between its establishment in 1941 and its liquidation in November 1984, Irish Shipping Ltd received in equity £129.5 million in constant 1985 prices. The company had fifteen years of profit to 1982 but lost £14 million in 1982–83. The company was liquidated because in August 1984 it had assets of £23 million and liabilities of £117 million. It was estimated that the total cost of keeping the company going for the period 1984–89 was £144.45 million, after which it would have debts of £59 million. The Minister for Communications stated in the Dáil that 'the present financial position of Irish Shipping Ltd is such that the company is unable to service any more borrowings. It is in fact insolvent without further financial support. Consequently the entire sum of £144.5 million which would be required to keep the company in operation in the period up to the end of 1989 would have had to be met by the Exchequer' (*Dáil Debates*, vol. 353, col. 2079).

The Minister also stated that Irish Shipping had between September 1979 and July 1981 entered into nine long-term speculative charter agreements with companies in Hong Kong and Jordan, which had proved disastrous. 'The charter agreements were entered into on behalf of Irish Shipping without the knowledge or consent of the then Minister for Transport or the then Minister for Finance and have led to the destruction of what was, up to then, a viable and successful State enterprise.'

Irish Ferries, operating between Ireland and the Continent, is the only section of the Irish Shipping group that has survived. Irish Ferries is the trading name of Irish Continental Group. It was owned by a subsidiary of Oceanbank Developments, which in turn was 75 per cent owned by Irish Shipping Ltd. In October 1987 National and City Brokers arranged for a number of institutional investors to acquire the company from Oceanbank.

Profits in the year to October 1988 were £869,000 on a turnover of £34.1 million. In 1989 the profits were £1.5 million on a turnover of £35.6 million.

The British and Irish Steam Packet Company Ltd (B and I Line) was acquired by the state in 1965 for £3.5 million; this is equivalent to £33.5 million at 1990 prices. Up to 1985 the equity invested in the company was £124 million at 1985 prices or £145 million at 1990 prices. At the end of 1989 the company had accumulated losses of £128.5 million, including a loss of £1.5 million in 1989. It received state equity of £42 million between 1985 and 1989, and had a capital deficiency of £26.5 million at the end of 1989.

The development of output, employment and company finances of the B and I Line in recent years is shown in table 19. Between 1985 and 1989 the turnover of the company declined by 38 per cent in money terms or 45 per cent in real terms. The number of passengers carried fell by 20 per cent and volume of freight by 17 per cent. The tangible fixed assets of the company fell by two-thirds from £38.5 to £12.7 million, and staff numbers fell by half, from 1,812 to 897.

The B and I Line owned three ships, with a combined gross tonnage of 11,761, and leased two more, with a gross tonnage of 12,353. The company claimed in 1989 the following market shares: RORO freight, 43 per cent; tourism (cars), 32 per cent; foot passengers, 32 per cent; and European LOLO freight, 21 per cent.

GOVERNMENT INTERVENTION IN SHIPPING MARKETS

The Green Paper on Transport Policy stated that 'the requirement of a strategic fleet derived from the experience of World War II when this country had to provide its own shipping resources.' While 'the relevance of a strategic fleet in an era of nuclear weapons might be questioned,' the Green Paper felt that it would be 'imprudent not to plan for less extreme forms of Emergency in which ships would be vital.'

The Green Paper stated that 'while some private sector shipping companies have shown admirable resilience in the face of the serious problems of the industry, the private sector generally lacks the resources necessary to take over the full responsibility for providing the necessary deep sea tonnage.' It listed the benefits of a 'commercially successful shipping fleet, in the areas of foreign exchange earnings, contribution to the balance of payments, employment, education and training of maritime personnel and the less tangible area of international prestige.'

Table 19

B and I Line output, employment, and financial situation, 1985–89

	1989	1988	1987	1986	1985
PHYSICAL					
Cars	162,000	150,000	125,000	135,500	166,800
Passengers	860,000	840,500	839,000	912,400	1,080,400
Freight tonnes	1,514,000	1,404,000	1,440,000	1,889,000	1,834,000
Employees (average number for year)	897	945	1,411	1,660	1,812
FINANCIAL	IR£000	IR£000	IR£000	IR£000	IR£000
Turnover	62,339	58,933	81,779	99,344	100,121
Loss before exceptional items	(1,508)	(2,840)	(10,675)	(6,756)	(6,601)
Loss for financial year	(1,462)	(1,535)	(19,953)	(15,356)	(29,601)
Tangible fixed assets	12,714	12,520	21,563	32,628	38,538
Share capital issued during year	4,800	6,200	11,000	20,000	5,000
Issued share capital at year end	101,500	96,700	90,500	79,500	59,500
Bank loans	28,809	31,334	34,121	33,529	23,039
Payroll costs (inc. UK and Europe)	17,650	16,850	22,700	25,200	26,600

Source: B and I Line (1989).

The Committee on Strategic Shipping Requirements in 1985 recommended a strategic fleet of 150,000 tonnes dwt, of which 140,000 tonnes would be deep-sea vessels 'for the transport of essential supplies in an Emergency'. In addition to incentives to investors, the Committee recommended
—that state agencies give a lead in greater use of Irish shipping services and control the choice of shipping services;
—that the IDA take steps to ensure that Irish shipping services get a better opportunity to compete for the provision of transport services for grant-aided industries; and
—that Irish ships be employed to the greatest extent possible to carry coal supplies to the ESB generating station at Moneypoint.

The degree of protectionism proposed by the committee is not explicit, because the costs would be hidden in higher electricity prices, reduced returns on the IDA's industry programmes, and control of the choice of shipping services by state agencies, leading to higher prices and taxes. Measures to reduce the cost of running shipping companies might make their services competitive in the market and attract business that currently uses non-Irish companies on the central and southern corridors to Britain as well as traffic using Northern Ireland ports and services. The services from Northern Ireland to Scotland attract traffic from the Republic to a competitive market between two private companies.

It appears to be an assumption underlying the acquisition by the state of the B and I Line that without it the customer would be worse off. According to the Green Paper, 'the Government, by acquiring the B + I Company in 1965, ensured that the State would have some influence over the adequacy and quality of shipping services on the Irish Sea. There is no doubt that the existence of an Irish controlled company has avoided the possible abuse of a dominant position where monopoly power could be exerted or service interrupted to the detriment of travel, trade and the economy generally.' This claim ignores the more attractive market result on the northern corridor, where such intervention did not take place. In fact for periods the B and I Line operated a cartel with Sealink, and its strike record was worse than Sealink's. In contrast to the £101.5 million share capital invested by the Government in the B and I Line between 1965 and 1990, Sealink was privatised for £66 million (stg) in July 1984.

The Government strategy of placing a state company in the market against Sealink assumed that the market itself would not generate competition at no cost to the taxpayer. It also ignored the effects of public finance on the efficiency of the body being subsidised. For example, the Green Paper notes that 'in the period 1979 to 1984, the company's annual financial charges grew by an estimated 41 per cent and labour cost per employee by 16 per cent in real terms.'

Various options for the future of the company were under examination in the middle of 1990, with privatisation being opposed by the trade unions.

OTHER SHIPPING MARKET POLICIES
In order to replace the former B and I Line service between Cork and Pembroke, a number of local authorities in south Wales and the Cork-Kerry area established Cork-Swansea Ferries in l987. The company received a state grant of £0.5 million when it began operations with a Polish chartered ship in April 1987, and a £300,000 grant in 1988. The service did not operate in 1989 but was revived in 1990 with a £0.5 million loan and a £0.5 million grant. The 1991 plan is for a £0.5 million loan only. The 1990 service operated from May to September and carried an estimated 100,000 passengers on a chartered Greek ship.

Since 1987 there has been a 25 per cent grant scheme for the purchase of new or second-hand ships up to seven years old. In addition, shipping qualifies for a 10 per cent rate of corporation profits tax. The fleet covered by these incentives has increased from 140,000 tonnes dwt in June 1987 to 183,000 tonnes in June 1990; this exceeds the recommendation of the Committee on Strategic Shipping Requirements. The cost of the 25 per cent grant scheme in 1990 was £1 million. The number of ships registered has increased from 66 in June 1987 to 76 in June 1990, an increase of 15 per cent compared, with the tonnage increase of 30 per cent.

AIRLINE DEREGULATION AND SHIP PASSENGER TRAFFIC
The impact of airline deregulation in 1986 on sea passenger numbers is shown in table 20. In 1985, the last full year of pre-deregulation air policies, sea companies had a 61 per cent market share, up 5 per cent from 1980. By 1989, however, the deregulated air industry had increased its market share to 61 per cent. In a

Table 20

Developments in air and sea shares of
Ireland–Britain travel market, 1980–89 (000)

(A) OVERSEAS VISITS BY IRISH RESIDENTS

	AIR CROSS-CHANNEL		SEA CROSS-CHANNEL	
1980	414	100	462	100
1982	335	81	496	107
1985	364	88	512	111
1986*	462	120	494	107
1987	596	144	488	106
1988	762	184	409	89
1989	832	201	411	89

(B) VISITORS TO IRELAND

	AIR CROSS-CHANNEL		SEA CROSS-CHANNEL	
1980	537	100	773	100
1982	537	100	804	104
1985	551	103	896	116
1986*	578	108	800	103
1987	768	143	787	102
1988	998	186	824	107
1989	1207	224	921	119

(C) TOTAL MARKET

	AIR	SEA	TOTAL
1980	951 (44%)	1235 (56%)	2186
1985	915 (39%)	1408 (61%)	2323
1989	2039 (60%)	1332 (40%)	3371
Index	214	108	154

* Airline deregulation occurred on 23 May 1986

Source: Central Statistics Office.

total market of 3.371 million passengers the sea companies carried only 72,000 fewer passengers in 1989 than in 1985, a fall of 5 per cent. The sea companies carried 8 per cent more passengers in 1989 than in 1980.

The air companies in 1989 carried 1.124 million more passengers than in 1985. Assuming that the 72,000 fewer ship passengers diverted to air, an estimated 6 per cent of the extra passengers carried by the airlines after deregulation were diverted from ships, and 94 per cent of the increase was generated traffic. The impact of airline deregulation in increasing the size of the market was much greater therefore than the traffic-diverting effect from the sea.

The deregulated market has obviously reduced the yield both for air and shipping companies. The cost structure of sea companies and existing airlines was protected in the years before deregulation and was therefore artificial. The sea carriers continue to do badly out of Ireland, with 101,000 fewer passengers carried in 1989 than in 1985. On the other hand 25,000 more visitors to Ireland used the sea in 1989 than in 1985. In 1989 the sea carriers had an increase of 97,000 passengers to Ireland, compared with an extra 109,000 visitors by air.

ROAD INVESTMENT

The National Development Plan, 1989–93, states that 'the major infrastructural deficiency relates to the internal transport network, particularly roads, which account for over 90% of traffic.' The plan goes on to state that 'the most significant reason for high Irish transport costs is the deficient state of the national roads and the access roads to the principal ports and airports. It is vital that road and rail costs should compare favourably with those in other Member States.' The plan proposes the expenditures on transport infrastructure shown in table 21 for the years 1989–93. Actual expenditures in 1989 were 92.4 per cent of the plan, and in 1990 are projected at 99.6 per cent of the plan,

3

Table 21						
Planned investment in transport infrastructure, 1989–93						
	1989	1990	1991	1992	1993	TOTAL
			£ million			
Roads						
—National	113	134	151	166.6	190.6	755.2
—Non-national	50	50	50	40	40	230.0
Rail and bus	7	10	10	9	9	45.0
Airports	24	29	31	24	12	120.0
Sea ports	15	20	15	11.5	10.5	72.0
Sea freight	6	9	16	19	15	65.0
Air channel	—	35	35	35	35	140.0
Total	215	287	308	305.1	312.1	1427.2
Total/GNP (%)	1.06	1.27	1.23	1.13	1.06	

Source: *National Development Plan, 1989*, p. 55; *ESRI Medium-Term Review, 1989–1984*, table A1.

excluding the Air Channel project. This project, involving air freight of goods to continental Europe, had not yet begun operations.

INTERNATIONAL INVESTMENT IN TRANSPORT INFRASTRUCTURE

The European Conference of Ministers of Transport (ECMT) annual report for 1987 found that Ireland in 1975 spent the lowest GDP share on inland transport infrastructure. Ireland then spent 0.6 per cent of GDP on transport infrastructure, compared with an ECMT average for eighteen countries of 1.5 per cent. By 1983, however, Ireland, along with Italy and Sweden, was no longer in the low-spending group and was close to the average (table 23 shows the ECMT data). A comparison with table 22 shows that by 1990 Ireland had become an above-average spender on transport infrastructure. In examining the share of investment allocated to transport infrastructure, the

3

Table 22			
Actual investment in transport infrastructure, 1989–90 (£ million)			
		1989	1990
Roads		164	184.5
Rail and bus		12.7	26.9
Airports		16	23.9
Sea ports		5.5	13.1
Sea freight		0.5	0.4
Air channel		—	—
Total		198.7	248.4
GNP		20,704	22,433
Transport infrastructure Investment/GNP (%)		0.96	1.11

Source: Public Capital Programme, 1990.

Table 23

Investment in inland transport infrastructure as a percentage of gross domestic product 1975, 1980, 1982–84

| | ECU current prices and exchange rates | | | | |
	1975	1980	1982	1983	1984
Austria	2.3	2.1	1.6	1.6	1.5
Belgium	1.9	2.0	1.7	1.3	1.2
Denmark	1.3	1.0	0.8	0.7	0.6
Finland	1.9	1.5	1.4	1.3	1.2
France	1.3	1.1	0.9	0.9	0.8
Germany	1.8	1.6	1.3	1.2	1.1
Greece	0.8	0.5	0.5	0.6	0.6
Ireland	0.6	0.7	0.9	0.9	0.8
Italy	1.1	0.7	0.9	1.0	1.0
Luxembourg	2.2	2.0	1.7	1.5	1.3
Netherlands	1.5	1.2	—	—	—
Norway	1.8	1.4	1.1	1.1	1.1
Portugal	0.9	0.7	0.8	0.7	0.6
Spain	1.5	0.8	0.9	1.0	0.9
Sweden	1.1	0.9	0.8	0.8	0.8
Switzerland	2.2	1.8	1.7	1.7	1.5
United Kingdom	1.0	0.7	0.6	0.6	0.6
Yugoslavia	2.7	3.0	1.9	1.8	1.8
Average	1.5	1.2	1.0	1.0	0.9

Source: ECMT Annual Report, 1987, p. 105.

ECMT reported that 'Ireland would seem to have been increasing it throughout the period under consideration.'

There are many problems in comparing the international data in table 23. For example, four of the high-spending countries—Austria, Belgium, Luxembourg, and Switzerland—have a substantial transit business shipping goods both produced and consumed elsewhere. The use of GDP in table 23 as a basis for comparing investment shares in transport infrastructure understates the share of available resources spent on transport infrastructure in Ireland. Net factor payments absorb 12.8 per cent of GDP in Ireland in 1990, so that GNP is a better measure of available national resources. GNP is used in tables 21 and 22.

GROSS DOMESTIC FIXED CAPITAL FORMATION
Investment in Ireland was £4,189 million in 1989 and £4,729 million in 1990; the transport investments in table 22 are therefore 4.7 per cent and 5.2 per cent of total investment in 1989 and 1990, respectively. The ECMT average in 1984 was 4.9 per cent.

Despite the widespread view that Ireland should invest more heavily in transport infrastructure, the country has not been an underinvestor in this category since 1982, and has latterly exceeded the European average.

APPRAISAL OF INFRASTRUCTURE INVESTMENT
In undertaking a programme of infrastructure investment, the appraisal procedures used are vital. In their assessment of the 1989–93 National Development Plan, Bradley and FitzGerald (1989) state that the ERDF road investment funds 'may result in higher inflation in the building industry, thereby reducing the volume of output achieved by a given expenditure set in value terms. We estimate that very rapid expansion, as contained in the Plan, is bound to generate some extra inflationary pressures, initially through profit markup and then through wage-push as skilled labour becomes scarce.'

Project selection is also important. In the late 1970s and early 1980s Ireland rivalled Japan with an investment-to-GNP ratio of over 30 per cent. The 1983 Public Capital Programme stated that 'our investment ratio (that is investment as a percentage of GNP) is one of the highest in the OECD countries. The results, in terms of growth and net employment creation, have been disappointing.'

Infrastructure investments must be accompanied by correct management and pricing policies; without these, infrastructure investments cannot generate an investment return. Thus there was no growth in traffic at Irish airports before deregulation, followed by extremely rapid growth afterwards. A policy change made loss-making infrastructures profitable. The loss of traffic by traditional ports to Larne, Rosslare and Dún Laoghaire has been a function of better service rather than of any difference in infrastructure.

The influence of the providers of infrastructure in persuading the state to purchase more of their products must also be recognised. The result for the providers of infrastructure is to have a road built. For society as a whole the important consideration is that the flow of benefits from a project should represent an adequate return on the investment cost. Investment is income to the infrastructure provider but a cost to society as a whole in the initial years of a worthwhile project and for longer in the case of a premature or incorrect project.

ROAD INVESTMENT APPRAISAL

The benefits of transport investments include: time saving for existing, diverted and generated traffic, as well as for traffic remaining on existing routes, which become less congested when other traffic goes to the new projects; vehicle cost savings, covering fuel, tyres, and brakes; and accident cost savings, where investments lead to higher safety standards.

Time saved permits the beneficiaries to engage in other activities. The saving of working time allows more goods and services to be produced with the labour released; the saving of leisure time permits existing activities to be extended or new activities to be undertaken. Savings in working time are normally valued at the average wage rate for the workers whose time is saved, together with the other elements of the total cost to the employer of hiring labour, including social insurance, employment taxes, and special allowances. Empirical tests would be necessary to see if savings in work time are in fact converted into extra output rather than extra leisure. Market forces are the means by which work time savings are converted into extra output. Companies that did not translate faster journey times into greater productivity of their transport operations would lose market share to those that did use time savings to the full.

Leisure or nonwork time savings are valued depending on the disutility of travel. Empirical studies have established that travel involved less disutility than work. Nonwork time savings are therefore valued at less than work time savings. Table 24 shows the various time savings values used in the British COBA evaluations of transport investment. The COBA programme calculates and discounts the costs and benefits of a road scheme over an assumed thirty-year life. It estimates both the net present value and the ratio of net present value to capital cost, using a 7 per cent test discount rate. COBA is not applicable where extensive redistribution and generation of traffic occurs. It is designed to measure the impact of removing a bottleneck on an inter-urban route. It is not applicable to urban road schemes, because of 'the intricacy of urban networks and traffic movements, the tendency for the increased supply of urban roads to generate substantial new demand which affects the level of congestion, and hence, costs for existing users; the competition from alternative modes of transport, especially acute

Table 24	
Value of time savings in Britain, May 1989 (p per hour)	
WORKING CAR	
Driver + 0.2 passengers	849.7
NONWORKING CAR	
Driver + 0.85 passengers	383.9
AVERAGE CAR	
14% working	
86% nonworking	468.8
LIGHT GOODS	
1 driver + 0.3 passengers	859.0
OTHER GOODS	
1 driver	622.5
PUBLIC SERVICE VEHICLE (BUS)	
1 driver	3,213.7
12.13 nonworking passengers	
0.007 working passengers	

Source: COBA 9 Manual, Department of Transport (Britain).

environmental problems, and a more sensitive interaction with land use' (Gwilliam and Mackie, 1975). COBA does not incorporate non-user costs such as noise, vibration, fumes, dirt, visual intrusion, physical severance, planning blight, loss of amenities, and disruption during construction. The Leitch Report (1977) recommended that separate statements on these impacts should be prepared. These should state the effects on pedestrians; the number of buildings to be demolished and farm units severed; the number of dwellings to be affected by noise, visual intrusion, and air pollution; the effects on local employment; community severance; and the impacts on environmental and natural assets.

Table 25 shows the estimated costs and returns on three programmes of investment in the National Primary Route Network over the years 1970–95, based on COBA. The main benefit from level of service D is time savings in raising operating speeds to a minimum of 56 km/h.

Table 25	**Costs and returns on investment in the National Primary Route rural network, 1970–95**		
	LEVEL OF SERVICE *		
	D	C	MID C
Total cost (1970 £ million)	219	316	423
Rate of return†	21%	14%	11%
Incremental rate of return‡	21%	7%	6%

* Level of service is based on US Highway Capacity Manual, 1965.
† With respect to the base condition, i.e. level of service E.
‡ With respect to the next-highest level of service, e.g. C over D.

Source: Barrett (1982).

A Department of the Environment economic evaluation method (based on a simplified version of the British COBA system) was used to provide a tentative assessment of sixty-one projects being considered for inclusion in this programme. The

Table 26	**Results of economic evaluation of proposed road investment projects**					
IRR	0–5%	6–10%	11–15%	16–20%	21–25%	25%+
Number of projects	13	17	14	11	3	3

Source: *Ireland: Road Development 1989 to 1993*, Dublin: Stationery Office 1989.

results are shown in table 26 and, while tentative, do serve to confirm that road development provides a positive economic return.

Tables 27 and 28 show the results of the evaluation of the Naas motorway bypass in 1984. Time savings dominate the project, because of the high proportion of work trips.

In comparing the actual and projected benefits from the Naas bypass for 1989, two alterations must be made in the assumptions underlying table 27: traffic volume, at 10,500, was 22.4 per cent less than the projections, and the route was accident-free, as in earlier years.

Time savings accounted for 90.5 per cent of the benefits from the bypass, or 18.6 percentage points of the 20.5 per cent internal rate of return on the project; fuel savings accounted for 2.6 per cent of the benefits, or 0.5 percentage points of the rate of return. A combined total of 19.1 percentage points of the benefits are therefore accounted for by time and fuel savings. Reducing these by 22.4 per cent to take account of the traffic shortfall therefore cuts the internal rate of return from 19.1 to 14.8 per cent in respect of these benefits.

The accident-free record of the bypass in 1989 and in earlier years increases the benefits under this heading from a base year value of £150,100 to £225,800: a 50 per cent increase. Accident cost reductions accounted for 6.9 per cent of the total benefits, or 1.4 percentage points of the 20.5 per cent rate of return. Raising this by 50 per cent brings the accident cost savings to 2.1 per cent and the total return for the traffic shortfall and better safety record to 16.9 per cent. This internal rate of return on the project is 18 per cent lower than the 20.5 per cent projected in table 27.

Table 27

Time stream of benefits and costs of Naas bypass with 20.51% discount rate (2% traffic growth and income growth assumed)

	TIME (£'000)	ACCIDENT (£'000)	FUEL (£'000)	TOTAL BENEFIT (£'000)	COSTS (£'000)
1983	2100.3	158.1	67.3	2325.7	16012.0
1984	1813.3	136.5	57.0	2006.7	10.0
1985	1565.5	117.8	48.2	1731.6	8.3
1986	1351.6	101.7	40.8	1494.1	6.9
1987	1166.9	87.8	34.5	1289.2	5.7
1988	1007.4	75.8	29.2	1112.5	4.7
1989	869.7	65.5	24.7	960.0	3.9
1990	750.9	56.5	20.9	828.4	3.3
1991	643.3	43.3	17.7	714.8	2.7
1992	559.7	42.1	15.0	616.8	2.2
1993	483.2	36.4	12.7	532.3	1.9
1994	417.2	31.4	10.8	459.3	1.5
1995	360.2	27.1	9.1	396.1	2.6
1996	310.9	23.4	7.7	342.1	2.1
1997	268.5	20.2	6.5	295.2	1.8
1998	231.8	17.4	5.5	254.7	1.5
1999	200.1	15.1	4.7	219.8	1.2
2000	172.8	13.0	4.0	189.7	1.0
2001	149.1	11.2	3.3	163.7	0.8
2002	228.5	9.7	2.8	141.3	0.7
Totals	14556.0	1095.7	422.6	16074.3	16074.7

Notes: The year begins on 1 October. Values are at 1983 prices. Fuel prices are assumed fixed in real terms.

Table 28

Sensitivity test results on rate of return on Naas Bypass

TEST	TITLE	SENSITIVITY TEST ASSUMPTIONS	RATE OF RETURN (%)
1	Basic	2% traffic growth, 2% income growth, fixed fuel price	20.51
2	Basic + fuel price rise	2% traffic growth, 2% income growth, fuel price growth	20.56
3	Zero value leisure	2% traffic growth, 2% income growth, fixed fuel price, zero value for leisure time	15.06
4	Zero growth 25% leisure	Zero traffic and income growth, 25% rate applied to 83% of cars in valuing time savings	12.75
5	Zero growth zero leisure	Zero growth in traffic and incomes, zero value for leisure time savings applied to 83% of cars	6.48
6	High time	Basic assumptions with time savings increased 25%	25.16
7	Low time	Basic assumptions with time savings decreased 25%	15.87
8	High accident value	Basic assumptions with accident costs increased 25%	20.86
9	Low accident value	Basic assumptions with accident costs decreased 25%	20.16

Source: Seán D. Barrett, 'A cost benefit analysis of the Naas motorway bypass', *ESRI Quarterly Economic Commentary*, January 1984.

The lower-than-projected traffic volume reflects the depressed conditions of the economy in the years immediately after the route was opened. The accident cost savings on the other hand are greater than projected because the route was accident-free, compared with British motorway accident rates of 0.273 fatal and 2.07 serious accidents for the projected volumes.

A number of environmental aspects of the Naas motorway were evaluated. It was found that traffic noise in Naas exceeded British target levels of 65 dB(A) both on the Dublin road and in the town centre, where the level recorded was 82.5 dB(A). The bypass transferred 10,000 vehicles a day from the town centre. Lead concentration in the air in Naas was comparable to that of central Dublin, as was smoke pollution, which in Naas was mostly caused by traffic. Other environmental aspects were that only one cottage was demolished in the construction, that in an area of housing the motorway was placed in a cutting to reduce noise and visual intrusion, that farm severance was minimised, and that adequate headroom was retained over the Naas branch of the Grand Canal, thus preserving this amenity. Similar benefits are to be derived from the Newbridge bypass according to the Road Development Plan.

Four alternative routes were examined for the Kilcullen link to the Newbridge bypass. The chosen route avoided disruption of the bloodstock industry and the archaeological area at Old Kilcullen. Kildare County Council also rejected routes that intruded close to historical houses.

The scientific study of the Kilcullen link noted that the motorway 'will consume approximately 180 acres of land. When viewed from a national perspective this loss is not significant in terms of impact on flora and fauna. There will however be localised impact on sites which are very interesting and contain rare species. The balance is somewhat redressed by the creation of large areas of land which are virtually inaccessible to the general public and provide ideal habitats for many species.' The main concern was the loss of wetland species through improved drainage.

TOLL FINANCE

The potential revenue from toll finance of the motorway sections of the 1970–95 road building programme is shown in table 29. At 1990 prices the toll required per vehicle-kilometre on motorways is 4.7p.

Table 29

Estimated motorway tolls, 1970–95
National Primary Route investment programme
at 1970 prices

LEVEL OF SERVICE	D	C	MID C
Motorway construction costs (£ million)	40.70	74.70	141.30
Annual cost including current	4.28	7.83	14.71
Vehicle-kilometres per day (million)	3.1	5.0	7.7
Break-even cost per vehicle-kilometre	0.4p	0.4p	0.5p

Source: Barrett (1982).

While tolls are common in the United States, France, and Italy, they are not an accepted part of motorway finance in Ireland or Britain. The Road Development Plan states that 'the Irish Government are satisfied that the scope for tolling is limited in this country because of our low traffic volumes by international standards and because only limited facilities suitable for tolling (ie motorways and river crossings) will be needed or provided.' The four projects listed for possible tolling are the Newbridge–Kilcullen bypass, the Dublin ring road, the Lucan–Kilcock bypass, and the downstream crossing of the River Lee. The Road Development Plan proposes the construction of 172 km of motorway by 1993, and all of this could be tolled. The Athlone bypass and the new Galway and Limerick bridges could also be tolled, because the time savings from such facilities are considerable.

In Britain the definitive case against tolls was made in a Ministry of Transport memorandum to the Trunk Roads and Motorways Estimates Committee in 1969. Collection costs and the potential diversion effect were the main reasons for rejecting tolls as a means of motorway finance. According to the memorandum, tolls are an 'indication only of the minimum benefit derived by the toll payer from the facility; in most cases the benefit would be considerably higher.' According to Sharp, the cost of converting the M1 to a toll route would be about 25 per cent of potential toll revenue. On the other hand the collection costs on the East Link Bridge in Dublin are only 10 per cent of toll revenue.

It is difficult to sustain the Ministry of Transport case against tolls. Costs of collecting revenue exist in all commercial activities; these could not exist were producers to avoid revenue collection costs by distributing their products free. If traffic diverts to a nonmotorway route to avoid a toll, the marginal utility to users of the motorway is less than the cost of provision, and other motorway programmes will have to be scaled down. Roads are no different from any other commodity, in that the price paid is 'only an indication of the minimum benefit derived by the toll payer from the facility'. Consumer surplus can exist for any commodity sold in the market.

The absence of tolls removes the price constraint on demand, as occurs for all priced commodities. Motorways cost significantly more than ordinary roads, and tolls communicate this to the motorway user. Without a price constraint, demand for motorways will be greater than with a toll. When roads are in plentiful supply relative to demands on them the problem of price is not urgent. This resembles land use where land is abundant relative to population. Land is treated as common property where the market price would be less than the cost of fencing off the land; as demand for land increases, however, a system of individual property rights will develop. The high cost of motorways and of road building in urban areas makes the case that it should also be priced. Motorways are expensive to provide, and their cost to users should reflect the fact.

URBAN ROAD PRICING
While paying for urban road space for parking vehicles has been accepted in most cities and large towns, charging moving vehicles has yet to gain wide acceptance.

The case for urban road pricing is that cars and other vehicles impose congestion costs on other vehicles, and significant costs on urban society as a whole in the form of air pollution, noise, vibration effects on buildings, community severance, planning blight, accidents, and visual intrusion. Where the social cost of an activity exceeds the private cost, a market system will produce too much of the activity generating the social costs. Road pricing would internalise the social costs by raising the price to include social cost. The Smeed Report (1964) estimated the congestion cost of an extra vehicle in London (table 30). A vehicle joining a traffic stream moving at 5 miles/hour (8 km/h) was estimated to impose marginal congestion costs of 88p per mile (55p per kilometre) on the other vehicles. At 20 miles/hour (32 km/h) the impact was much less, at 2p per mile (1.2p per kilometre). Prices have increased tenfold since the Smeed Report.

A full system of road pricing would incorporate all social costs in the price. The Smeed Report ignored the costs imposed on nonmotorists. Off-vehicle monitoring and in-vehicle meters have been proposed as pricing systems. Road pricing has been described as having 'an impeccable academic pedigree' by Gwilliam and Mackie (1975); but only one example of area

Table 30	
Estimated congestion cost per extra vehicle, 1962	
TRAFFIC SPEED (MILE/HOUR)	MARGINAL CONGESTION COST (p/MILE)
5	88
8	30
10	17
12	11
15	6
20	2

Source: Smeed Report (1964).

licensing has been carried out. In Singapore, area licensing operates in the central business district. Cars entering the supplementary licensing area must pay an additional licence fee of $25.80 for permission to enter between 7:30 and 10:15 a.m. A reduction in traffic of 33 per cent was obtained, compared with a target of 25 per cent (Barrett and Walsh, 1983). The Singapore charging system indicates that the internalisation of the externalities arising from urban motoring can reduce the social costs involved, through car pooling, transfer to bus, transfer of journeys to off-peak times, and division of through trips away from city centres.

The cost of the Smeed proposals was estimated at £5 to £10 per metre per car and £5 million for pricing points in central London (these figures would have to be increased tenfold to obtain 1990 costs). Investment and road pricing are alternative responses to the urban congestion problem. Pricing allocates urban road space efficiently by pricing out the marginal users. Investment plans in 1983 in the Dublin area alone provided for the expenditure of £800 million on roads and £500 million on rapid rail.

Bus lanes, by reserving a portion of the road for the bus, which is an efficient user of scarce road space, are a substitute type of road pricing system. Unfortunately in Dublin there is a low level of enforcement of this and other traffic and parking legislation. The penalties imposed, together with the low prospect of enforcement, are not sufficient to deter widespread illegal parking.

Management of urban road space requires the co-ordination of police, local authority and public transport operators. This has been difficult to achieve, and the Dublin Transportation Authority, set up for this purpose, was subsequently abolished.

In the Irish case the alternatives to using road pricing to achieve optimal use of urban road space are increasing congestion, expensive investment in new infrastructure, public transport subsidies, or a combination of all three. In Ireland an investment approach has dominated a management approach to solving urban congestion. While the 1989–93 Road Development Plan relies heavily on EC funds, the high ratio of public debt to GNP and the high Irish tax burden on average incomes indicate that such schemes will have to be reduced if EC funding is curtailed. Of the £762.2 million cost of the programme over the years 1989–93, £560.7 million is to be funded from EC sources.

The proposal in the Road Development Plan for the expenditure of £9,000 million on roads over a twenty-year period would in the early years mean allocating 1.74 per cent of GNP to road investment (Road Development Plan, table 3).

Ireland is already a heavy spender on transport infrastructure. A danger in increasing this further, even if largely through EC funding, is that the provision of infrastructure might absorb an unduly large share of national resources, to the detriment of the directly productive sectors of the economy. The overhead and administration costs of the road programme in 1986 were £51 million, according to the Statistical Abstract for 1989. The overlapping structures of central and local government require examination.

THE NATURE OF INFRASTRUCTURE RE-EXAMINED
Hirschman (1958) distinguished social overhead capital and directly productive activities. 'Social Overhead Capital is usually defined as comprising those basic services without which primary, secondary and tertiary productive services cannot function. In its widest sense it includes all public services from law and order through education and public health through transportation, communications, power and water supply, as well as such agricultural overhead capital as irrigation and drainage systems. The hard core of the concept can probably be restricted to transportation and power.'

Infrastructure services are thus basic to other activities; are typically provided by public agencies, or private agencies under public control; are either free or sold at regulated prices; cannot be imported; and are characterised by 'lumpiness' (technical indivisibilities) as well as a high capital output ratio, provided the output is at all measurable.

Economic changes since Hirschman defined the concept indicate that infrastructure can be increasingly provided in the market sector. Capital lumpiness and intensity is no longer a barrier to market provision, and the distinction between social overhead capital and directly productive activities has been blurred. Utilities such as water, telephones, gas, airlines, airports, bus and road freight operations and ports and shipping have been transferred to the private sector, and the issues have typically been oversubscribed. Toll roads and bridges are a commercial activity. Airports and seaports face competition from Northern Ireland and British rivals. Reserve charges make Telecom Éireann a competitor with other telephone systems. Gas and electricity interconnectors would make these products tradable goods and undermine the nonimportability characteristic of infrastructure.

Where infrastructure is priced, user revenues and producer costs determine whether the project will attract investment. Thus in 1990 Guinness Peat Aviation offered to finance a £2,000 million investment in European air traffic control. While formerly such investment might be thought of as solely for the public sector, there is no market reason for the underinvestment in air traffic control. It is paid for by airlines and recouped from passengers.

Many factors, such as growth of the availability of private funds, changes in technology, and privatisation, have blurred the distinction between infrastructure and directly productive investment. Increasing the supply of infrastructure is naïve if this is undertaken in the hope that infrastructure alone will generate economic activity to make optimal use of the infrastructure.

A further consideration in evaluating an infrastructure investment programme is the likely demand for that infrastructure. The published figures on vehicle numbers show a sharp reduction in growth in the 1980s compared with earlier decades. Petrol sales have also fallen over the period 1980–88.

THE REDUCTION IN TRAFFIC GROWTH
The number of vehicles registered increased by 84 per cent in the 1960s, 63 per cent in the 1970s, and 12 per cent from 1980 to 1989 (table 31).

Car numbers in the 1980s showed only a 5 per cent growth. The favourable tax treatment of cars adapted for the goods category by removing seats and blocking out side windows may

Table 31				
Vehicles under licence				
	CARS	GOODS VEHICLES	BUSES	ALL VEHICLES*
1960	169,681	43,530	1,436	302,767
1970	389,338	48,751	2,012	558,403
1980	734,371	65,052	2,722	911,031
1989	773,396	130,020	3,834	1,019,560

* Includes above categories plus motorcycles, tractors, taxis and hackneys, exempt and 'other vehicles'

Source: Department of the Environment.

have diverted some demand for cars into the goods vehicle category. If we assume that 'normal' commercial vehicles grew by 35 per cent in the 1980s as in the 1970s, approximately 42,000 cars were adapted as commercial vehicles in the 1980s for tax reasons. This adjustment increased the growth of car numbers in the l980s to 11 per cent, compared with 89 per cent in the 1970s.

Petrol sales declined by 18 per cent between 1980 and 1988, indicating that total car distances travelled and average distances per vehicle have fallen. The reduction in petrol sales was 226 million litres. Feeney and Hynes estimated average fuel consumption for cars in Ireland at 11 km per litre. The reduction in petrol sales therefore translates into a reduction of 2,485 million car-kilometres between 1980 and 1988. The total of vehicle distances in 1979 was 19,014 million km, and the reduction over the period 1980–88 was 13 per cent. The increased sales of 217 million litres of diesel would not affect car distances, because Feeney and Hynes found that 96 per cent of cars ran on petrol. The information is not available to translate the diesel sales rise into vehicle-kilometres increase.

Table 32		
Road fuel consumption, 1980–88 (million litres)		
	PETROL	DIESEL
1980	1,362	421
1981	1,372	428
1982	1,321	432
1983	1,232	446
1984	1,193	474
1985	1,150	516
1986	1,146	569
1987	1,130	592
1988	1,137*	638

* Includes 1.4 million unleaded

Source: Revenue Commissioners, annual reports.

The governor of the Central Bank of Ireland warned (Annual Report, 1989, p. 78) that 'there is a risk of too much attention being paid to the size of the Structural Funds and not enough to the quality of the investments they will finance. Much of our present public finance problem is due to our having invested in capital projects which do not, in fact, service the borrowings involved. Efficient use of the Structural Funds is crucial for Ireland to be able to take full advantage of EMU [economic and monetary union].'

The warning in the Irish case is appropriate, given the tradition of wasteful investment, high administration costs, a reluctance to charge tolls, and a decline in road use as measured by petrol sales.

THE REGULATION OF ROAD TRANSPORT

REGULATION OF THE BUS INDUSTRY
The restriction of competition between bus operators in Ireland was begun under the Road Transport Act, 1932. The object of the legislation was to protect the railways, which had lost market share because of road competition. Protectionism gained popularity over competition in economic policy in the later 1920s and early 1930s. Conroy (1928) believed that 'it would not be inconsistent with this age of "trusts" and "combines" that all competition in the transport world should be eliminated ... Road Transport should be merely used as a complement for rail transport, not as a substitute for it.'

Rail passenger traffic on the Great Southern Railways declined from 15.5 million in 1926 to 11.9 million in 1931. This company was created in 1924 by the amalgamation of all railway companies operating entirely within the Irish Free State. From 1926 onwards there were frequent complaints that the railways suffered unfair competition from road competitors. Shields (1937) found that by 1927 'numerous privately owned commercial road services, unfettered by legislation had begun to entrench themselves as public road carriers.'

The Road Transport Act, 1932, prohibited the operation of scheduled passenger transport services except under licence from the Minister for Industry and Commerce. The Act permitted railways to acquire road transport companies. In the Dáil the Minister for Industry and Commerce, Mr McGilligan, stated that while the tendency in the Act was 'to divert traffic into the hands of the three transport companies operating on a big scale at present ... we do allow for the existence side by side with these three agencies of the independent bus proprietor or company. Personally, I would look forward to seeing these people disappearing by degrees either by process of amalgamation with other companies or by the main companies deciding that their future lay in certain areas in the country and leaving other areas for exploitation by independent bus operators' (*Dáil Debates*, 1932).

4

The local monopolies that the 1932 Act sought to create, and their acquisitions of the independent bus services, are shown in table 33. There were 1,098 acquisitions of independent bus services by the railways and the Dublin United Tramways Company, which was granted monopoly status in the Dublin area. A small number of bus services licensed under the 1932 Act were not acquired by the railways; they operated mostly in remote areas and on a small scale. The biggest concentration of the remaining independents was in the Kilkenny-Tipperary-Waterford region.

The Transport Tribunal of 1939 estimated that the 1932 Act reduced the number of passengers carried by the independent bus operators from 34.5 million to 1 million per year. The market share decline was from 46 to 0.92 per cent.

The Milne Report (1948) found that there were twenty-eight independent bus operators. 'These licences are issued at the discretion of the Minister and in practice have only been granted in cases where there was no public service and no existing operator was prepared to provide one. No new entrant has been granted a licence since 1940.'

The Beddy Report in 1957 found that there were also '28 small operators holding passenger licences in respect of regular omnibus services.' It estimated that they carried 1.2 million passengers in 1955.

The Green Paper on Transport Policy in 1985 found that there were thirty-eight private companies licensed to operate over 105 routes. 'Most of these routes were short rural services. Regular services (e.g. daily, weekly) are provided on 70 routes while occasional services (e.g. trips to seaside, dances etc.) operate over the remaining 35 routes.' The Green Paper stated that 'the general policy has been to refuse an application for a licence where there is an existing CIE service or a service by a licensed operator, unless it can be shown that the proposed service would meet a need not being met by the existing service.'

In the Dáil in 1979 the Minister for Industry and Tourism stated that in the previous two years eleven applications for new passenger road licences were refused, because the existing services were judged to be adequate. The Minister stated that CIE was consulted in every case and that he did not consider that there would be any justification for an appeal to an

Table 33

Transfers of independent bus service licences to statutory transport companies, 1933–41

	TO GSR		TO GNR		TO DUTC		TOTAL	
	Voluntary	Compulsory	Voluntary	Compulsory	Voluntary	Compulsory	Voluntary	Compulsory
1933	459*	1	5	12	–	–	464	13
1934	157	55	1	1	18	47	176	103
1935	11	191	4	78	–	–	15	269
1936	1	9	–	–	–	5	1	14
1937	2	17	1	–	–	–	3	17
1938	2	–	–	–	–	–	2	–
1940	1	–	–	–	–	–	1	1
1941	1	2	–	–	–	–	1	12
							663	419

* 446 licences held by a subsidiary company up to 31 December 1933

GSR: Great Southern Railways. GNR: Great Northern Railways. DUTC: Dublin United Tramways Company.

Note: There were no transfers in 1939. Transfers to remaining railway companies were 10 in 1934, 3 in 1935, and 3 in 1938.

independent arbitrator. The lack of a right of appeal, and the practice of supplying CIE with the applicants' market research, caused a lack of confidence in the system, and the independent operators chose a different development path in the 1980s.

TRAVEL CLUBS

Barrett (1982) noted that it was Government policy to resist the extension of the independent bus services to routes linking the principal towns. 'There has, however, been a recent growth in travel clubs using charter bus services as a way around the restrictions on bus transport.'

The Green Paper noted that 'there are operators who provide what are regular service type operations using "private hire", through "travel club" arrangements, as a basis for claiming immunity from the requirements of the road transport legislation. Despite successful prosecutions, business has increased over the years and the services are now well established.' Conlon stated that 'the number of unlicensed weekend operators doubled between 1983 and 1986 while the number of unlicensed daily services have trebled in the same period. In 1986 there were 56 operators with 115 vehicles operating unlicensed weekend services and 44 operators with 68 vehicles operating unlicensed daily services.' Assuming forty passengers per bus, a return journey per day per bus on weekday service or six days per week and a weekend service throughout the year there were 850,000 passengers in 1986 on the daily services and 478,000 on the weekend services, making a total of 1.3 million. This compares with an estimated 519,000 in 1983, an increase of 64 per cent in three years.

The Green Paper presented the arguments for and against liberalisation of bus services as set out in table 34. It stated that 'the increased use of "private hire" operations, which are not provided for in the legislation, is a manifestation of the need for review.' Because CIE provincial bus services had been given 'a much more commercial mandate' there was not 'the same justification for preventing competition by the private sector'. A further factor influencing the need for review of the legislation was that 'the original objective of the 1932 Act to protect the railways has not been realised.'

The Green Paper case against bus deregulation is that it involves a reduction in safety, loss of an integrated network,

Table 34

Arguments for and against liberalisation of bus services

FOR

Customers would benefit from competition in fare levels and quality of service.

Market supply would adjust to passenger demand, thereby producing more effective and economical use of transport resources.

Would challenge CIE and its staff, giving them an opportunity to respond to competition in the market.

A licensing system would provide a means for controlling the very considerable transport operations that are at present legally doubtful.

Would encourage experiments with minibuses and small buses, particularly as replacements on routes where the use of large buses is uneconomic due to low levels of demand.

Success of private operators would help to convince CIE to withdraw from certain areas (or services), thereby leading to improved CIE financial performance: also increased competition might help the railways to be more cost-effective.

AGAINST

Risk that unrestricted competition would adversely affect the quality of service, with safety implications.

Full liberalisation might lead to gaps in service rather than an integrated network.

Operators would concentrate on routes with high demand, leaving CIE to serve the low-demand routes.

Benefit of cross-subsidisation within CIE would be eroded, as CIE reduced fares on well-supported routes in oder to retain traffic.

Possibility of reduction in CIE staff on foot of a fall in demand for CIE services, with redundancy and other cost implications.

Competition would reduce CIE's share of bus traffic, in the short term at least, and possibly cause a further fall in rail passenger traffic levels. This would adversely affect CIE's financial position, and could lead to its having to reduce costs (by eliminating and/or reducing uneconomic services).

Source: Green Paper (1985), p. 23.

loss of service on thin routes, loss of cross-subsidisation, and loss of demand for CIE services.

Safety of vehicles is a matter for the Public Service Vehicle (PSV) Office of the Garda Síochána, and the abolition of this office has not been proposed.

The passenger will decide whether the bus service should be run as a single entity rather than on a point-to-point basis. There is no evidence of substantial passenger transfers between routes at present. Many of the licensed private operators and hire services operate in remote areas, because neither CIE nor the Great Southern Railways wanted to serve such places. These include Cavan, Monaghan, Donegal, north Kerry, and west Cork, from which the railways withdrew.

Cross-subsidisation means the charging of some passengers above long-run marginal cost and others below. This creates the risk that passengers so overcharged will cease to pay this form of tax and that areas with low car ownership will have to cross-subsidise little-used services elsewhere. Lower-cost producers will be able to serve more remote areas without cross-subsidisation.

What happens to CIE's traffic in a deregulated market depends on how the company reacts to the new environment. There is substantial evidence from airline deregulation in the United States and between Ireland and Britain, and from bus deregulation in Britain, that this has stimulated improvements in efficiency by established operators.

BUS COMPETITION IN 1990
On most long-distance routes to Dublin the de facto deregulation of bus services has provoked a competitive response from Bus Éireann, even where this involved competition with Iarnród Éireann. The pattern of this competition is normally that CIE, road and rail, decides to 'take on' an independent operator by selectively cutting fares and increasing frequency. For example, in July 1988 Bus Éireann followed private operators Cronin and O'Mahony onto the routes from Cork and Tralee to Dublin. CIE has the advantages of national marketing and identified city bus depots in meeting this competition. On the other hand, there is little evidence of economies of scale in bus operation, and local operators may be better placed to meet local market needs.

In other respects, however, there is no level playing field in public policy towards the independent bus service in Ireland.

For example:

—CIE had an annual subsidy of £110 million in 1989. The Bus Éireann accumulated deficit over the period February 1987 to December 1989 was £9.9 million; the Dublin Bus deficit was £19.1 million. These deficits are in addition to state grants of £10.4 million to Bus Éireann and £45.4 million to Dublin Bus. Thus in a period of just under three years the two CIE bus companies incurred losses and received subsidies of £84 million.

—CIE borrowings are part of the public sector borrowing requirement. This reduces the cost of funds by two percentage points and increases the supply. By contrast, many independent bus companies use hire purchase.

—CIE receives first option on the school transport contract, worth £31.2 million in 1989. CIE then decides how much it wishes to subcontract to the private sector—a reversal of the case normally made for nationalisation.

—Where CIE's competitors seek an extension to a route or a new route for individual stage carriage these proposals are sent by the Department of Tourism and Transport to CIE rather than assessed by an independent authority. There is no right of appeal against the decisions, and CIE has the benefit of its competitors' market research, as well as the right to pre-empt the new service by going on the route itself.

—Only the minority of CIE's competitors that have stage carriage licences are permitted to carry old people in the free travel scheme. CIE gives the department a discount of 40 per cent on these passengers; most of the independent bus services offer larger discounts but are not permitted to serve this market, which in 1989 cost £26.1 million.

DEREGULATION OF THE BUS SERVICE

The National Development Plan (1989–93) promised to 'replace the outdated Road Transport Act, 1932. The planned changes will bring in the liberalisation of the bus transport industry to provide greater competition and increased flexibility in the range of services.'

The deregulation of British bus services has been phased over three stages. Long-distance coach services were deregulated in 1980; local bus services, excluding London, were deregulated in October 1986; while the deregulation of bus services in London was deferred, according to the White Paper *Buses* (p. 14), to allow time for the operation of institutional changes such as the transfer of London Transport from the Greater London Council and permission for private firms to apply to the traffic commissioners rather than face a London Transport veto.

INTERCITY COACH SERVICES

Fares fell by 35 to 40 per cent following the deregulation of intercity coach services (ECMT, 1988, p. 10), and seven hundred new services were introduced (*Buses*, p. 11). The White Paper also found (p. 30) that 'the NBC National Express services have been dominant in this area, the number of passengers carried increasing by 45% between 1980 and 1983.'

Dominance of the market by National Express increased when its largest competitor, British Coachways, withdrew in 1983. Since 1983, prices have continued to rise in real terms, and by 1985 'in aggregate, prices were slightly lower in real terms than immediately before deregulation. This fall in real price marks a departure from previous trends. In the past the regulated bus industry has been characterised by slow productivity growth which has been associated with rising real costs and prices' (Jaffer and Thompson, 1986, p. 62). They conclude that 'the introduction of competition in sectors formerly the preserve of state monopolies is worthwhile,' but that 'effective competition requires an effective competition policy' (p. 65).

The main barriers to competition in the deregulation of intercity coach services were the exclusion of new entrants from coach stations owned by the National Bus Company (NBC), the market power of the NBC of operating in markets without freedom of entry until the deregulation of local bus services in 1986, and the weak bankruptcy constraint of the NBC as a public company.

Coach stations were subsequently sold separately from the NBC, and the market outside London was deregulated. The privatisation of the NBC removes the bankruptcy constraint. The problem of market dominance was tackled by selling the NBC as fifty-two separate bus companies, six coach operating companies, and eight engineering companies; and in addition National Express, National Travelworld and the coach station subsidiary were also sold as separate companies (Vickers and Yarrow, 1988, p. 374).

Beesley (1989) states that 'NBC's ability to harass competition (through National Express) was even greater than the commentators appreciated.' Its nationalised status was a help in pursuing what would be judged by most anti-trust standards as 'competitive dubious practices'. Vickers and Yarrow (p. 374) found that the 'National Express policy bears some sign of a campaign of predatory pricing but, whether or not this is so, the competition authorities stood by and did nothing.'

Since 1985 transport in Britain has lost its exemption from the Restrictive Trade Practices Act. It faces investigation by the Office of Fair Trading (OFT) in matters such as fares collusion between bus companies. 'The crunch will come if and when OFT decides that remaining agreements are restrictive and proceeds to their determination by the Restrictive Practices Court' (Beesley, 1989, p. 35). The Monopolies and Mergers Commission in the case of the merger between Badger Line and Midland West declared the merger to be expected to operate against the public interest. The parties to the merger were companies that were sold off separately after the Transport Act, 1985.

THE DEREGULATION OF LOCAL BUS SERVICES IN BRITAIN
The local bus sector, excluding London, was deregulated in October 1986. A study by the Transport and Road Research Laboratory (TRRL) of the first year of deregulation (Balcombe, Hopkins, and Penet, 1988) found the following results:
—some increase in bus-kilometres;
—about 85 per cent of vehicle-kilometres being operated commercially;
—fares largely unaffected by deregulation as such;
—some loss of services (later mainly restored);
—initial reduction in patronage;
—a reduction in subsidies;
—a substantial increase in the number of operators;
—greater competition between operators;
—innovations, such as the use of minibuses;
—no change in safety standards.

The ECMT Round Table on 'The Role of Government in a Deregulated Market' (Beesley, 1989) updated the TRRL findings from the first year of bus deregulation. The Transport Statistics Great Britain (TSGB) series of the British Department of Transport also provides information on the first two years of deregulation.

(1) *Bus-kilometres:* In 1987/88 there were 2,342 million local stage bus-kilometres, compared with 2,076 million in 1985/86, the last full pre-deregulation year; the increase was therefore 13 per cent. The 1987/88 output reversed a decline throughout the 1980s in this measure of output (TSGB, table 2.36).

(2) *Commercial service:* 349 million vehicle-kilometres out of the total of 2,343 million were provided under subsidy. The separation of the commercial network from the social service network ensures that subsidies are used only on routes where the service would not be provided commercially (TSGB, table 2.37).

(3) *Fares:* The fares index for all operators with a base year of 1985 = 100 increased from 110.1 in the July–September quarter in 1986 to 112.7 in January–March 1987. These quarters are the periods before and after deregulation in October 1986 (TSGB, table 2.38).

(4) *Service:* The loss of service did not persist throughout the first year. There were 2,076 million vehicle-kilometres in 1985/86 and 2,160 million in 1986/87 (TSGB, table 2.36).

(5) *Patronage:* The number of passengers carried was 5,641 million in 1985/86; it declined to 5,332 in 1986/87, and increased slightly to 5,340 million in 1987/88 (TSGB, table 2.37). Before deregulation the number of passengers fell from 6,864 million in 1977 to 5,461 million in 1985/86.

(6) *Subsidies:* Revenue support grants for bus companies increased from £225 million in 1979/80 to £465 million in 1985/86. After deregulation they declined to £365 million in 1988/89 (TSGB, table 1.19). The ECMT report shows that the bus subsidy in cities outside London has been reduced from £201 million in 1985/86 to £117 million in 1987/88. In the nonmetropolitan counties of England there was a reduction in operating subsidies from £86 million in 1985/86 to £67 million in 1987/88. Beesley (p. 29) found that outside London 29 per cent of contracted subsidised services were provided by private operators.

(7) *Operators:* The ECMT estimates that there were 5,600 operators in the private sector before deregulation. In the first months

after deregulation there were 350 new entrants. Following further market entry there was a net increase of 465 operators in May 1988.

(8) *Competition:* The increase in competition is reflected in the extra bus-kilometres and in the increase of 465 (8 per cent) in the number of private operators.

(9) *Innovations:* In 1980 small vehicles with up to 35 seats comprised 8 per cent of the fleet of 69,100 vehicles. By 1985/86 they accounted for 14 per cent of the fleet of 67,900 vehicles. After deregulation the small-bus fleet increased to 15,900, or 22 per cent of a fleet of 71,700 (TSGB, table 2.40).

(10) *Accidents:* The accident rate per 100 million vehicle-kilometres for buses and coaches was 395 in 1980, 333 in 1986, and 292 in 1988. For all vehicles the rates were 152 in 1980, 129 in 1986, and 120 in 1988 (TSGB, table 2.48). Taking 1980 as an index, the accident involvement rate both for buses and all vehicles declined to an index of 84 by 1986. Since bus deregulation its accident rate has fallen further to 74 while for all vehicles the rate has fallen to 79.

PRODUCTIVITY
The output of the bus sector in terms of vehicle-kilometres increased by 13 per cent, as seen under point 1 above. The staff employed decreased after deregulation from 174.3 thousand to 158.8 thousand, a decline of 9 per cent; there was thus a 24 per cent increase in bus-kilometres per staff member. The White Paper *Buses* (1984, p. 12) claimed that 'after careful review of all the evidence, the Government has concluded that the potential exists for cost reductions of up to 30 per cent of total costs of public operators.'

The pattern of the reduction in employment was that the number of drivers and conductors declined by 2 per cent, maintenance workers by 26 per cent, and other staff by 22 per cent between 1985/86 and 1987/88. Beesley offers as the explanation for this that 'deregulation, it seems, represented a credible threat to rents enjoyed by labour under regulation. Arguably, the most formidable strongholds of union power were in maintenance and in the urban areas. Yet in two years the Metropolitan PTC's shed 41 per cent of their maintenance staff ... Presumably maintenance was contracted out instead.'

In London, deregulation was postponed from 1986 to the early 1990s. The White Paper (p. 14) stated that 'the need to take a grip on subsidy has led the Government to take over responsibility for the London Transport Executive and reconstitute it as London Regional Transport.' This new authority was required to contract out work wherever suitable. It allowed bus operators to apply to the traffic commissioners to run bus services rather than depend on the agreement of London Transport. 'The Government has decided, in these special circumstances, to defer deregulation in London, while the changes, so recently instituted, bear fruit.'

In September 1989 Robinson (1989) found that 'some 25 per cent of the London Regional Transport bus network has been put out to tender and this will go on rising. London Buses has pushed its success rate for winning LRT tendering out services to 50 per cent.' In preparation for privatisation, London Bus has been split into twelve local companies with their own managing directors and boards.

IMPLICATIONS FOR IRELAND OF BRITISH COACH
DEREGULATION
In the first stage of express coach deregulation in Britain the dominant NBC pursued a policy of maximisation of output in order to drive out the new entrants. Analyses of the period 1980–83 indicate predation by NBC on its rivals, but Britain lacked a mechanism to apply competition policy to the transport sector. Nor was it possible to ensure that the subsidised and unsubsidised sections of NBC were entirely separate. NBC was also able to pursue its policies without the risk of bankruptcy, whereas the new entrants competed without subsidy in an industry that received subsidies that increased from £224 million in 1979/80 to £465 million in 1985/86. With the privatisation of NBC in many units and the change to competitive tendering for subsidies designated for social services, some of the barriers to contestability have been removed. It remains to be seen, however, just how the Office of Fair Trading, the Restrictive Practices Court, the Monopolies and Mergers Commission and the Competition Policy Directorate of the EC will promote contestability in the bus sector.

In the light of British experience it appears unlikely that the fare wars between Irish private-sector bus operators, CIE rail and CIE bus could have been sustained at the fares charged during the summer of 1989 without causing bankruptcy in the private sector and a rise in the CIE deficit. Fares such as £5 return between Dublin and Rosslare are significantly below Bus Éireann's costs. In 1988 the Bus Éireann services outside the city routes produced 46.2 million vehicle-kilometres of bus travel, at a cost of £66.8 million or £1.45 per vehicle-kilometre. Rosslare to Dublin is 161 kilometres, and a £5 return fare, assuming forty passengers per bus, would generate revenue of 61.3p per vehicle-kilometre. This is a revenue-to-cost ratio of 42.3 per cent. The round trip would generate costs of £473 and revenues of £200.

IMPLICATIONS FOR IRELAND OF BRITISH LOCAL BUS DEREGULATION

CIE's bus-kilometres declined by 5.0 million (2.3 per cent) between 1980 and 1989. There is no indicator of commercial or social services provided, despite Government regulation of the sector since 1932. Real fares per passenger increased by 16 per cent between 1980 and 1989; the number of passengers declined by 9 per cent. The bus service overall was in profit until 1972 and increased its losses between 1980 and 1989, from £21.6 million to £22.5 million. CIE has not responded to the increase in the use of minibuses in Britain. In 1989 in its fleet of 2,237 buses there were 56 minibuses, or 2.5 per cent of the fleet. Even under Ireland's restrictive laws on competition in transport there has been a growth in potential and actual competition for some market segments. In 1980 the CIE bus fleet was 2,440, or 90 per cent of the national bus fleet of 2,722. In 1989 it was 2,237, or 58 per cent of the national fleet of 3,834.

The gains from the deregulation of British local bus services in reducing subsidies, increasing productivity, increasing availability of services and increasing innovations all appear possible in Ireland, given the track record of the monopolistic provision of bus services in the years 1980–89 outside the limited number of routes on which there was competition. As in Britain, there appeared to be within CIE a policy of charging lower fares on routes with competition than without and in below-cost selling on the former routes. Ireland has yet to apply competition policy to transport. It is not possible to ensure that public subsidies to transport are not diverted into below-cost selling on routes with competition or into higher costs overall. The National Development Plan (1989–93) provides for the inclusion of Articles 85 and 86 of the Treaty of Rome in national law. These articles outlaw price fixing and the abuse of dominant position.

The deregulation of London bus services after the local bus services elsewhere in Britain was a result of the timing of administrative changes in local government in London in the middle 1980s. Competitive tendering was introduced and the London Bus company split into twelve companies before privatisation. Beesley (1989, p. 25) reports that 'London Regional Transport itself formally embraced a policy of welcoming deregulation in 1987, undoubtedly with the hearty agreement of the Chairman of London Buses Ltd., who has made no bones about its importance in helping his drive towards greater labour productivity and the need to reorganise London Buses into independent management units.' The London experience does not therefore support the exclusion of Dublin from deregulation of Irish bus services.

IMPLEMENTING BUS DEREGULATION
The British experience affords useful guidelines on how to deregulate the transport market without incurring the excess costs of monopoly and predatory pricing. The object of deregulation is to ensure that the bus industry performs with maximum efficiency. This requires competition both in the market and for services that are deemed to be social services.

WITHDRAWAL OF BUS ÉIREANN SUBSIDY
In the year of deregulation the Book of Estimates should not provide a subsidy for Bus Éireann. This sector of the bus industry is likely to be the one that will at first experience the greatest impact from deregulation. There is evidence of substantial de facto competition in this market segment at present; this cannot take place on efficient terms if one producer retains a state subsidy.

The withdrawal of the Bus Éireann subsidy will require the company to decide whether to continue to provide a service or withdraw. The list of withdrawn services will provide the Department of Tourism and Transport for the first time with a statement of where Bus Éireann at present incurs losses. Were the company to retain all its services following the withdrawal of subsidies there would be an immediate gain to the taxpayer from bus deregulation of about £6.8 million in 1991. The fuel rebate for public transport should either be abolished or provided for all operators; because of the administrative costs involved, the abolition of the rebate should be favoured.

DIVISION OF CIE INTO STAND-ALONE COMPANIES
In addition to the withdrawal of the Bus Éireann subsidy to ensure efficient competition between Bus Éireann and other operators, it will be necessary to prevent the seepage of the general CIE subsidy into the bus sector. While administrative methods to confine the CIE subsidy to the railways are possible, such arrangements are complex and difficult to enforce. It is suggested therefore that CIE be disestablished and that Iarnród Éireann, Bus Éireann and Dublin Bus become legally separate entities.

COMPETITIVE TENDERING FOR THE SCHOOL BUS SERVICE
In a deregulated market the school bus service should also be open to full competition. The present situation whereby Bus Éireann both administers the service and is one of its potential operators has an inbuilt bias in the company's favour. This places Bus Éireann in a position of potentially cross-subsidising competitive scheduled services from its school bus monopoly powers. Indeed, part of the defence of the present school bus service is that competitive tendering would impose losses on Bus Éireann compared with the present system.

APPLICATION OF COMPETITION POLICY TO TRANSPORT UNDERTAKINGS
Competition policy improved overall economic efficiency by ensuring that anti-competitive practices do not occur. Thus, for example, articles 85 and 86 of the Treaty of Rome forbid price collusion and the abuse of a dominant market position. The proposed Competition Bill will apply these policies in Irish national law. While transport has enjoyed exemptions from competition law in Ireland and the EC, these exemptions do not have a sound economic foundation. The Competition Bill should not exempt transport from its provisions.

Price collusion between bus operators is no more desirable than elsewhere in the economy. The abuse of a dominant position either by overcharging or undercharging should not be permitted in transport. The former is an abuse of the consumer, while the latter is an abuse of the competitor. Similarly, mergers in transport should be subject to the same scrutiny as those in other fields in order to assess their effects on market competition, and anti-competitive mergers disallowed.

COMPETITIVE TENDERING FOR SOCIAL SERVICE SUBSIDIES
Where the market does not provide a service and such a service is deemed to be socially necessary, it should be provided by public tendering for the service and not by deficit funding as at present. After the end of the tendering period a further round of tenders should be sought so that the incumbent does not assume property rights to the service and retains an incentive to efficiency.

ALL OPERATORS SUBJECT TO A BANKRUPTCY CONSTRAINT
The ending of deficit funding and across-the-board subsidies ensures that only subsidies that are 'earned' in competitive tendering are paid to bus companies. If a bus company fails to earn enough to cover its costs in its receipts for both commercial and social services it must face a bankruptcy constraint. The use of subsidies to finance fare wars on competitive routes is impossible under the system proposed here. This was a feature of the British intercity bus deregulation in the years 1980–83.

THE DESIGN OF A DEREGULATION PACKAGE
The measures proposed in this section show the difficulties involved in deregulating a sector efficiently. The examples from US airline deregulation and British bus deregulation show that existing large firms require the stimulus of new entrants, but that the new entrants face predation, geographical price discrimination, use of public subsidy to finance fare wars and the absence of a bankruptcy constraint in responding to the incumbents. This package is designed to obtain and retain the benefits of competition.

THE DEREGULATION OF ROAD FREIGHT
In September 1988 the process of deregulating the Irish road freight sector was completed. Quantity controls on market entry, in force since 1933, were replaced by quality controls over

professional competence and good repute and financial standing. The objective of quantity licensing in 1933 was to protect the position of the railways; the main effects, however, were to promote own-account haulage at the expense of hired haulage and to attach a scarcity rent value to haulage licences.

The Road Transport Act, 1933, restricted the operation of road freight for reward, outside small exempted areas around the major towns, to those operating before the passing of the Act. The existing carriers were restricted in their areas of operation, types of merchandise carried, and weight and number of vehicles. The Act provided for the acquisition of hauliers by the railways, by compulsory purchase if necessary. Through the Act it was hoped 'to make it possible for the Great Southern Railway in its area and other railway companies in their areas to establish themselves in what is described as a monopoly position' (*Seanad Debates*, vol. 16, par. 979). The number of hauliers declined from 1,356 before the Act to 886 in 1938. Restrictions peaked in 1956, when the Transport Act decreed that vehicle leasing was equivalent to licensed haulage and therefore subject to the 1933 law.

A later review (Pacemaker Report, 1963) stated that 'when the [1933] Act was passed it was doubtless intended that all private hauliers would be bought out. The process of buying-out stopped however, and those unacquired thus found themselves in that position more or less by accident.'

The process of liberalisation began in 1970. The carriage of cattle, sheep and pigs was deregulated. Weight, area and commodity restrictions were removed, and extra vehicle licences were awarded to the national carriers. There were then 840 national hauliers. In 1978 each licence holder was permitted to operate six vehicles per licence; but the ban on new entrants except by licence purchase remained. The Transport Consultative Commission recommended deregulation in 1981; this was resisted by the licence holders, but the legislation was passed in 1986, with a two-year transition period.

The liberalisation of the freight market has brought about three important shifts in market share. Road freight has increased its market share compared with rail; within road haulage, hired haulage has increased compared with own-account haulage; and within the hired haulage sector the independent operators have increased compared with the road fleets of the railway companies.

Table 35

Market shares in Irish road freight (%)

YEAR	OWN ACCOUNT	HIRED
1964	83	17
1980	60	40
1985	55	45
1986	52	48
1988	48	52

Source: Green Paper (1985); Central Statistics Office, Road Freight Series.

Table 35 shows that since 1964 and the CSO Survey there has been a steady increase in the hired haulage share of road freight. Table 36 shows that the independents have increased their share of hired haulage at the expense of the road fleets of railway companies. Table 37 shows that the rail share of all freight movements in Ireland is small.

The expansion of hired haulage by the independents can be seen under a number of headings. From 1970 to 1987 they have increased their kilometres run from 48.4 million to 258.3 million. Tonnes carried rose from 5.8 million to 25.8 million. Receipts increased from £4.5 million to £155.4 million and staff from

Table 36

Market shares of independent hauliers (%)

	1970	1985	1988
Kilometres run	100	151	154
Tonnes carried	61	93	97
Vehicle numbers	49	88	92
Staff employed	38	82	86
Receipts	44	88	192

Source: Irish Statistical Bulletin.

Table 37	Road and rail freight market shares (%)	
YEAR	RAIL	ROAD
1960	22	78
1965	16	84
1970	16	84
1975	16	84
1980	11	89
1985	12	88
1988	10	90

Source: CIE annual reports; Central Statistics Office, Road Freight Series.

1,851 to 4,934. Average size remains small, and only 167 of 1,203 operators had six or more vehicles in 1987.

For students of public policy, road freight regulation provides a classic example of a policy with completely unintended effects. The object of protecting the railways was not achieved. Instead, the policy gave road haulage licences a scarcity rent value and promoted the growth of own-account freight transport.

Table 38 shows the comparative development for licensed hauliers and railway companies in the road freight market from 1970 to 1987 in terms of kilometres run, tonnes carried, vehicles, staff, and receipts.

Table 39 shows the categories of goods moved by road in 1980 and 1988. Apart from a strong export performance, much of the economy was in recession for most of the period, and this is reflected in the stagnation of overall freight volumes and the decline in most sectors other than foreign trade.

TAXI LICENSING
Quantity licensing in transport results in a scarcity value for the transport licence. For example, a road haulage licence was estimated to have a market value of £12,000 in 1980; this is the equivalent of £25,700 at 1990 prices. Since deregulation a haulage licence has no market value; but sectors such as Dublin taxis remain tightly regulated.

Table 38

Licensed hauliers' and railway's shares of road freight, 1970–87

	KILOMETRES RUN (MILLION)		TONNES CARRIED (MILLION)		VEHICLES		STAFF		RECEIPTS (£ MILLION)	
	H	R	H	R	H	R	H	R	H	R
1970	48.4	29.5	5.8	3.9	1,051	1,101	1,851	2,999	4.5	5.7
1980	144.2	18.5	12.9	2.2	2,386	673	3,778	1,334	63.8	13.6
1985	197.3	12.7	17.0	1.4	2,810	368	4,166	906	115.8	15.5
1987	258.3	10.6	25.8	1.2	3,507	304	4,934	791	155.4	14.2

H: licensed haulier. R: railway.

Source: *Irish Statistical Bulletin.*

Road freight activity by traffic category, 1980–88 (tonne–km)

	1980	1988	Index*
Total	5010.5	4999.6	100
Import/export work	867.6	1401.6	162
Livestock	83.5	89.7	107
Farm produce from farms	356.1	220.5	64
Fertilisers, feed etc. to farms	273	256.4	94
Deliveries to road works and building sites	946.7	608.5	64
Deliveries to retail outlets	1177.7	936.2	79
Deliveries to wholesalers	471.2	413.9	88
Deliveries of materials to factories	355.5	369.4	104
Deliveries to households	126.5	94.6	75
Other works and unspecified	362.7	602.0	166

* 1980 = 100
Source: Central Statistics Office, Freight Transport Survey, 1988.

Table 40 shows that the cost of a Dublin taxi plate in 1990 was £43,000, compared with only £3,500 in 1980, when the taxi service was examined by the Transport Consultative Commission. No additional taxi licences have been issued, and the number has remained at 1,835 (Carriage Office data). The existence of a scarcity value for the licence indicates that under a deregulated system, monopolistic rents and charges would fall and output would increase.

The body responsible for determining the number of new taxi licences is Dublin City Council, and the licensing body is the Garda Síochána Carriage Office.

The arguments for and against quantity licensing have been reviewed in the discussion on air transport, buses, and road freight. The case for quantity licensing of taxis is particularly weak, since taxis have no obligation to provide 'social services'

Table 40	
Sale price of Dublin taxi plate, July 1980–90	
1980	£ 3,500
1981	£ 7,750
1982	£ 5,600
1983	£ 5,500
1984	£ 6,750
1985	£ 7,200
1986	£12,000
1987	£17,000
1988	£23,000
1989	£35,000
1990	£43,000

Source: *Evening Press* classified advertisements.

or to operate to a timetable. All forms of quantity licensing enjoy the strong support of the licence holders, and the regulatory authorities are 'captured' by the industry. Thus, for example, a 1977 National Prices Commission report concluded that 'for the current level of demand there are too many vehicles licensed to operate. Continuation of the trends of the last two or three years will lead to a predominance of part-time operators. This assists neither the public or those who are committed to earning their livelihood solely as taxi drivers.' The reason why an industry with demand fluctuating by time of day should require supply only in units of full working days is not stated by the commission.

Further examples of this regulatory approach are seen in the recommendations of the Transport Consultative Commission to the effect that checks for whether a taxi was 'on the road' the minimum number of hours should be introduced, that regulations should prescribe the times at which a part-time operator could work, and that taxis be limited 'to three or four specified models of the larger and comfortable class'.

In the light of the decade of experience of deregulation since these recommendations of the National Prices Commission and the Transport Consultative Commission, there is no case for the measures proposed. The supply of taxis should be as flexible as the demand; it is immaterial to the user how the taxi driver spends his off-peak hours. Government intervention to confine taxis to three or four large vehicles raises costs. Consumers trade off price and quality in virtually every other purchase they make, without Government intervention to raise costs.

The rapid growth of the price of a taxi licence in Dublin shows serious and increasing inefficiency in the licensing system. It is recommended that the ban on new entrants be removed, without a transition period, and that the powers of Dublin City Council to decide the number of taxi licences be removed. Quality licensing would remain under the control of the Carriage Office.

NORTHERN IRELAND SHARED TAXIS

The shared taxis in west Belfast, north Belfast and Derry are an important case study of the development of taxi services in a deregulated market.

In 1984 it was estimated that the shared taxis carried 1.7 million passengers in Derry, 15.6 million in west Belfast, and 5.6 million in north Belfast (Barrett and McLoughlin, 1984). The fares charged were the same as on buses in some cases and up to 37.5 per cent lower in others; for example from Belfast to Twinbrook the bus fare was 56p and the taxi fare 35p.

The non-price advantages of the shared taxis are greater frequency, longer hours of operation, shorter journey times, the ability to bypass congestion on the route, and the ability to provide door-to-door service for old people, invalids, and passengers with children and shopping. In a survey of user attitudes by Derry Taxi Association the principal advantage of shared taxis was the helpfulness of the taxi drivers with old people and children: 95 per cent of those surveyed found the taxi drivers more helpful than bus drivers.

In north Belfast the shared taxi fleet was expanded experimentally to include minibuses. Passengers preferred the comfort of the taxis, and the minibuses were sold.

On the Falls Road it is estimated that the market shares in terms of public passenger numbers are about two-thirds for taxis and one-third for buses. The Shankill Road estimates are three-quarters for taxis and one-quarter for buses. No market share estimates are available in Derry.

A further advantage of the shared taxis is that no public subsidy is required. This would normally be the case in western Europe for a system with this number of passengers in urban areas.

REGULATORY POLICY

The operators of the shared taxi services in Northern Ireland have experienced opposition on several occasions from government agencies. There have been periodic advertising campaigns by the Department of the Environment against the services. The operators believe that their PSV tests by the Department of the Environment are tougher than those for buses, and that their importance in public transport is not acknowledged in the allocation of street space for city centre terminuses.

In 1978 the Report of the Public Inquiry into the Belfast Urban Area Plan Review of Transportation Strategy (the Lavery Report) recommended 'the elimination of black taxi competition with the bus services', because the taxis had 'no obligation to provide services at uneconomic times or on uneconomic routes.' In the light of subsequent experience, these complaints against the taxis were unfounded. The taxis operate longer hours than the bus service, and the six-seater taxi is obviously more economic on thin routes than a fifty-seater bus.

While the attitude of local government has changed from opposition to tolerance, the operators feel that extensions of the system to other areas and towns would cause further opposition from the authorities. Yet signature campaigns by taxi operators have been successful in showing the support for the services in their areas, and legal proceedings against the services by the authorities have not been successful.

NEW URBAN PUBLIC TRANSPORT AND REGULATION

Public transport by road in urban areas has typically offered only a choice between a high-fare, regulated taxi system and the conventional bus service, usually a monopoly and heavily loss-making.

Attempts to bridge the gap in the market between the conventional taxi and bus include shared taxis, minibuses, jitneys, and a variety of paratransit. Such systems are frequently found in developing countries but have been displaced by regulation in the developed world. The Northern Ireland experience of shared taxis indicates that regulatory reform could entice new suppliers to public transport with products attractive to consumers and not requiring public subsidy.

In 1983 Associated Minibus Operators Ltd (AMOS) applied to London Transport for permission to operate four routes with sixteen-seater minibuses. The positive experience of shared taxis in Northern Ireland notwithstanding, the application was refused. Traffic inspector T. G. Holden turned down the proposals, on the following grounds:

(1) The routes and terminals were not defined precisely. No provision was made for waiting at terminals.

(2) Diversions from the route to avoid traffic jams were 'unacceptable, partly because of doubts about the legality and partly because of the general passenger confusion that would arise.'

(3) The 'stop anywhere' proposal was neither safe nor practicable, except possibly in the suburbs.

(4) Supervision and control: 'The limited provision for supervision of the operation (equivalent to two supervisors per route) would be quite inadequate.'

(5) Traffic congestion: 'There would be some adverse effect upon traffic congestion—difficult to quantify and perhaps small.'

(6) The bulk of the traffic would be drawn from existing public transport services.

(7) The minibus service might not be financially viable.

(8) Disintegration of services: 'There would be no through ticketing, no attempt to serve railheads or passenger interchanges and no concessionary fares.'

(9) Safety: 'The operation proposed would be substantially less safe than existing services,' because of pressure on drivers to maximise earnings, and inadequate control over vehicle and maintenance standards.

(10) The services were not in the public interest. Differences in speed and comfort were unlikely to be significant. The services 'would add to congestion, would be damaging to amenity in some ways, would cause inconvenience and danger by stopping anywhere, and by diminishing the revenue of competing services would lead to increased subsidy, higher fares or the reduction

or withdrawal of services to the public not in competition with the AMOS routes.'

The shared taxi service in Northern Ireland has not caused the above problems. It shows that:

(1) Terminals are not a problem. Passengers typically wait in the taxis, which move off when there are six passengers.

(2) Diversions from a fixed route to avoid traffic jams, far from causing passenger confusion, are seen as a consumer advantage by passengers.

(3) The 'stop anywhere' policy has not been a cause of accidents.

(4) The inspector's opinion that two supervisors per route would be 'quite inadequate' is not borne out by experience. Each of the Northern Ireland systems is run by a manager, with some clerical assistance. There are three managers for the 23 million passengers, rather than supervisors appointed for each route.

(5) Traffic congestion is difficult to analyse, because of the security situation in Belfast and Derry. Nonetheless the services have attracted car owners where buses have traditionally failed.

(6) Abstraction of traffic appears to have taken place, but there has been a welfare gain to consumers in increased frequency and standard of service, and some fare saving.

(7) The service has been financially viable.

(8) Disintegration of services: The shared taxi services serve the main bus terminus for long-distance services in Derry and the second rail terminus in Belfast. There is no through ticketing; but this is hardly a disadvantage if 23 million passengers prefer cheap point-to-point transport. The shared taxi services have available the full range of concessionary fares without subsidy.

(9) Safety: Drivers do not exercise inadequate control over vehicle and maintenance standards. They face regular PSV tests on their vehicles and the quality controls set by their associations. There is no evidence that the services are 'substantially less safe than existing services'.

(10) The public interest: Shared taxis are superior to buses in speed and comfort. Under a more liberal licensing regime it is likely that the services would expand in response to requests from residents of areas not now served by shared taxis.

The experience in Northern Ireland commends the shared taxi idea to those resigned to increasing subsidies for urban public transport. A higher standard of service has been provided in a difficult regulatory environment. The fears expressed by Inspector Holden about this type of innovation in urban public transport are groundless if one takes into account the Northern Ireland precedent. In the difficult economic and security situations of Belfast and Derry ordinary people of initiative and enterprise, without degrees in transport economics but alert to the transport requirements of their neighbours, have brought about a significant improvement in urban public transport.

Arguments against paratransit are a tradition in the industry but are a restraint on developing competitive, efficient urban public transport.

THE PERFORMANCE OF PUBLIC TRANSPORT IN 1989

In 1989 CIE comprised three major loss-making businesses—Iarnród Éireann, Bus Éireann, and Dublin Bus—which accounted for 92 per cent of its expenditure. The group made profits in road freight, catering, and the operation of Rosslare Harbour; it had smaller loss-making businesses in tours, a ferry service to the Aran Islands, and consultancy.

CIE had a deficit in 1989 of £100.3 million (table 41). It was financed by a state subvention of £109.8 million. Each of the CIE businesses will be examined and an overall assessment made of the organisation.

5

Table 41	CIE expenditure, revenue, and deficit, 1989 (£ million)		
	EXPENDITURE	REVENUE	DEFICIT
Railways	153.5	72.0	81.5
Dublin Bus	90.7	74.9	15.8
Bus Éireann	77.9	73.9	4.3
Aran ferry	0.6	0.1	0.5
Road freight	18.3	18.8	(0.5)
Tours	3.7	2.8	1.0
Rosslare Harbour	2.9	4.8	(1.9)
Catering	4.7	4.9	(0.2)
Consultancy	0.5	0.4	(0.2)
	352.8	252.5	100.3

Note: ( ) denotes profit.

The financial position of the railways in 1989 is shown in table 42. Total costs were £153.5 million. The revenues from customers at £72.0 million covered 46.9 per cent of costs; this compares with customer revenues of 48 per cent of total costs in 1980 and 79 per cent in 1969/70 (McKinsey Report, 1981, p. A11).

Table 42	Railway revenue and expendiutre, 1989 (£ million)		
	MAINLINE	HOWTH–BRAY	TOTAL
Customer receipts	63.3	8.6	72.0
Expenditure	127.6	25.9	153.5
Revenue/cost ratio (%)	49.6	33.2	46.9
Source: CIE Annual Report, 1989.			

RAILWAY OUTPUT, RECEIPTS, AND COSTS

Railway output, measured in passenger-kilometres and freight tonne-kilometres, rose by 7 per cent between 1980 and 1989 (table 43). Passenger traffic increased by 18.2 per cent, while freight declined by 10.3 per cent.

During the 1980s real receipts per railway traffic unit continued to fall. Between 1980 and 1989 there was a fall of revenue per passenger unit in real terms of 16 per cent and per freight unit of 14 per cent (table 44). Real freight revenues per unit fell 50 per cent between 1970 and 1979 (Barret, 1982, p. 94). Unit passenger revenues fell by one-third during the 1970s (McKinsey Report, 1981, p. A10).

Between 1980 and 1989 railway costs per traffic unit rose faster than customer receipts per unit (table 45). Cost per unit rose by 62 per cent, while revenues rose by 60 per cent. The widening gap was bridged by an increase of 63 per cent in the deficit per traffic unit.

The consumer price index increased by 103 per cent between 1980 and 1989. The growth in unit costs on the railways was thus 60 per cent of the growth of consumer prices as a whole, but revenue per traffic unit increased by only 58 per cent of the

5

Table 43				
Railway output, 1980–89 (million traffic units)				
	PASSENGER–KM	FREIGHT T–KM	TOTAL	INDEX
1980	1,032	624	1,656	100
1981	994	678	1,672	101
1982	887	654	1,541	93
1983	846	582	1,428	86
1984	903	601	1,504	91
1985	1,023	601	1,624	98
1986	1,075	574	1,649	100
1987	1,196	563	1,759	106
1988	1,180	545	1,725	104
1989	1,220	560	1,780	107

Source: CIE Annual Reports.

growth in consumer prices. Table 46 shows the changes in railway revenues between 1980 and 1989.

If freight unit prices had been maintained in 1989 at 1980 real values the freight income of the railway would have been £3.4 million greater. If the passenger fares had been held in real terms

Table 44		
Railway receipts per traffic unit, 1980–89 (p)		
	Per freight t–km	Per passenger–km
Receipts in 1980	2.00	2.22
1980 receipts at 1989 prices	4.06	4.51
Actual 1989 receipts	3.51	3.77
Index (1980 real price = 100)	86	84

Source: CIE Annual Reports.

Table 45

Railway unit costs and revenues, 1980–89

	1980	1989	INDEX
Railway costs (£ million)	90.5	153.5	170
Customer receipts (£ million)	40.8	72.0	176
Traffic units carried (million)	1,656	1,780	107
Cost per unit (p)	5.5	8.9	162
Revenue per unit (p)	2.5	4.0	160
Deficit per unit (p)	3.0	4.9	163

the revenue would have been £8.8 million greater. The miscellaneous income of £5.3 million in 1980 is worth £10.8 million at

Table 46

Railway receipts, 1980–89 (£ million)

	PASSENGER FARES	FREIGHT	TOTAL*	INDEX
1980	22.9	12.5	40.7	100
1981	24.2	15.5	45.4	112
1982	26.9	17.5	49.9	123
1983	28.9	17.3	52.3	129
1984	32.4	17.9	56.8	140
1985	37.3	18.5	62.5	154
1986	38.6	18.8	63.3	156
1987	41.0	18.7	66.6	164
1988	44.0	18.7	69.3	170
1989	46.0	19.5	72.0	177

* Includes miscellaneous receipts, which increased from £5.3 million in 1980 to £6.5 million in 1989, an increase of 23%.

Source: CIE Annual Report.

1989 prices; this is £4.3 million more than the actual increase in the period 1980–89, and is a fall of 40 per cent in real terms.

The combined impact on the three categories of maintaining 1980 real prices in 1989 would have been an extra £16.5 million of railway revenue, an increase of 22.9 per cent on the £72 million actually obtained.

Railway costs rose 70 per cent between 1980 and 1989. This comprised a 62 per cent increase in the cost per unit and a 7 per cent increase in the traffic units carried. If railway unit costs had risen at the same rate as railway revenues there would have been a saving in 1989 of £1.9 million.

THE MARKET FOR MAINLINE RAIL TRAVEL

Passenger traffic on the mainline rail system peaked at 8.1 million journeys in 1979, declined to 6.5 million in 1983, and recovered half of the lost journeys to reach 7.3 million in 1988. There were 7.6 million journeys in 1989.

McKinsey forecast a broadly static market for mainline rail traffic in the 1980s, with population growth the only source of traffic increase. In the McKinsey survey of passengers, 43 per cent gave as their reason for travelling by rail that there was no alternative available. This outscored by a factor of four the passenger perceptions of the traditional advantages of rail, such as speed, comfort, and being less tiring than driving. 32 per cent of passengers gave fare reductions as their preferred change in service on the railways (table 47).

In the 1990s railways will face additional competition from bus deregulation, which will reduce the railway share of captive budget-sensitive passengers. The number of daily unlicensed bus services trebled between 1983 and 1986, and the number of weekend services doubled (Conlon, 1988). These services thus carried 1.3 million passengers in 1986, assuming forty passengers per bus trip. Trying to hold on to price-sensitive passengers will put pressure on CIE to reduce costs or to seek higher subsidies and capital write-offs.

The new regional airports at Sligo, Knock, Galway, Kerry and Waterford will reduce rail travel on the part of those who previously went by train to Dublin, either as a destination or a starting point for an onward journey by air. Domestic air travel grew 67 per cent in 1988 and 34 per cent in 1989 to 675,000 passengers.

Table 47

A profile of the mainline rail passenger, 1980

(A) PRIMARY REASON FOR CHOOSING RAIL, BY JOURNEY TYPE (%)

No alternative means available	43
More economical / less expensive	10
Fast journey time	11
Suitable departure / arrival times	11
Less tiring than driving	11
Comfortable / pleasant / can move around	10
Part of package / group travel	2
Company policy to travel by train	2
Other reasons	1

(B) POSSIBLE ALTERNATIVE MODES CHOSEN HAD RAIL BEEN UNAVAILABLE (%)

Car	37
Bus	25
Taxi	1
Other means	11
Would not have travelled	25

(C) CHANGES IN SERVICE MOST REQUESTED (%)

Cleaner trains	15
Better catering	12
More trains	12
More punctual trains	4
More comfortable carriages	6
Less expensive / cheaper fare	32
Faster trains	9
More convenient departure / arrival times	4
Don't know	6

Source: McKinsey Report (1981), appendix 3, tables 12, 18, 28.

Between 1981 and 1988 the number of private cars registered fell from 775,000 to 749,000. While part of the decline in car numbers was caused by the reintroduction of motor tax in 1981, the reduction in personal consumption also reduced the role of the car as a competitor with the passenger train. The ESRI Medium-Term Outlook forecast of a volume increase of a quarter in personal consumption between 1988 and 1994 indicates that a growth in car numbers is likely to replace the decline over much of the 1980s.

Rising real incomes may generate some increase in business travel by rail as the opportunity of driving increases. However, McKinsey found that only 15 per cent of rail passengers were travelling for business. The other reasons given were 'leisure' (60 per cent of total), 'personal' (15 per cent), and 'personal nondiscretionary' (10 per cent).

DUBLIN SUBURBAN RAIL: HOWTH–BRAY
In 1989 this service had an income of £8.6 million and total costs of £25.9 million, and received grants of £17.2 million. Its revenue-to-cost ratio was 33.2 per cent, compared with 49.6 per cent on the mainline system and 46.9 per cent on CIE rail as a whole. The number of passengers carried was 15.0 million, a decline of 2 per cent on 1987. The average fare per passenger was 56p, compared with £4.64 on the mainline system.

The 1984 Annual Report of CIE noted that 'passenger carryings on the DART system averaged 40,000 per day by the end of 1984. It will require to carry 80,000 daily to cover operating costs. It is anticipated that this figure will be reached by 1988.' Passenger numbers have increased from 32,000 per day in 1985 to 42,000 in 1987, before returning in 1988 to the 40,000 of the initial running period in 1984. Several feeder bus services have been withdrawn, because of lack of custom. In 1989 the service generated £8.6 million in passenger fares and received £5.9 million in operating grants and £11.3 million in interest subsidy. To cover its operating costs would require a 69 per cent increase in revenues, while to cover also the interest cost would require a threefold increase in revenues.

The DART service replaced a previous diesel train service, which carried 5.4 million passengers in 1983 and an estimated 8.8 million in 1979. Extensive track work between 1980 and 1983 contributed to the loss of 3.4 million passengers from the Howth–Bray system.

The capital-intensity of DART can be seen in its revenues in 1985, its first full year of operation, of £11.7 million on an investment of £113 million at 1984 prices. By comparison, the assets employed by CIE in 1983, the last full pre-DART year, were £220 million, with customer revenues of £195 million.

The capital cost of DART was financed by borrowings from the European Investment Bank (£54 million) and domestic banks (£59 million). EMS interest subsidies of about £3 million and an ERDF grant of £11.3 million were received by the exchequer for the project. The finances of DART depend significantly therefore on interest rate movements. For example, in 1989 the grant for DART interest was £11.33 million. However, in 1987 the Government interest grant was £15.26 million, or 35 per cent greater than in 1989.

The results of DART improved in 1989 over 1987, even though 2 per cent fewer passengers were carried (table 48). Since 1980 real fares per passenger on the Howth–Bray service have increased 37 per cent, real costs per passenger by 18 per cent, and the deficit per passenger by 4 per cent. The revenue-to-cost ratio was 27 per cent in 1980; it fell to 23 per cent in 1987, but as lower interest rates reduced capital charges in 1989 the revenue-to-cost ratio rose to 33 per cent.

Table 48			
Receipts and costs of the Howth–Bray train service, 1980–89			
	1980	1987	1989
Receipts (£ million)	1.6	7.4	8.6
Cost (£ million)	5.9	30.4	25.9
Deficit (£ million)	4.3	23.0	17.3
Revenue/cost ratio (%)	27	24	33
Per passenger			
Receipts (£)	0.20	0.48	0.56
Cost (£)	0.75	1.99	1.72
Deficit (£)	0.55	1.50	1.16

THE EXTENSION OF DART

The Transport Consultative Commission report on passenger transport services in the Dublin area examined four major investment programmes in public transport. These were two rapid rail schemes, a semi-metro system, and a scheme combining diesel trains and a busway; table 49 summarises the main findings. Alternative D—the train-plus-busway option—would cost between 36 and 42 per cent of the more expensive options but would give a public transport share in the city centre at peak hours of over 99 per cent of those generated by the more expensive options. The costs in table 49 are stated in 1979 prices. However, the 1985 Green Paper on Transport Policy (p. 34) estimated that the cost of implementing the rapid rail options in the Dublin Rapid Rail Transit Study (DRRTS) would be 'of the order of £750m.'

The Transport Consultative Commission's report (1980, appendix 13) indicated the main adjustments it made in the

Table 49	Transport Consultative Commission evaluation of public transport strategies in Dublin, 1980			
PLAN TITLE	A RAPID RAIL	B RAPID RAIL	C SEMI- METRO	D DIESEL/ BUS
Capital cost (£ million 1979)	266	222	264	94
Public transport peak share* (%)	61.9	6.17	62.4	61.8
Increase in public transport at peak over D* (%)	0.43	0.11	1.05	base
Net present value (1973 £)†	49.9	40.2	35.4	35.9
Benefit/cost ratio	2.02	2.12	1.76	4.86

* Refers to city centre area between 08:00 and 09:30 and 17:00 and 18:30.
† In the 'Net present value' calculations a test discount rate of 7% was used.

Source: Transport Consultative Commission (1980), ch. 11.

estimated costs of the DRRTS in 1975. The Howth–Bray signalling costs were double the DRRTS estimates. Electrification costs were 90 per cent greater than the estimates. In addition the commission recommended that the DRRTS estimate of rolling stock costs should be increased by 20 per cent and that the operating cost estimates should be doubled.

Alternative D was supported in the National Development Plan (1989–93), which announced the introduction of new diesel train commuter services to the area west of Dublin on existing railway lines. The planned expenditure was £26 million, including new rolling stock, upgrading of signalling, and the opening of eight commuter stations (p. 50). The Government decision was adversely commented on by the chairman of CIE in the 1988 accounts (p. 4): 'Regretfully, I have to report our deep disappointment at the level of support for Public Transport, particularly in relation to the development of our National Railways, requested in the National Development Plan 1989–93 submitted to the European Commission in March this year.'

The four alternatives examined were:

(A) Rapid rail on Howth–Bray with new lines to Blanchardstown, Ronanstown, and Tallaght; busways to Finglas and Leopardstown.

(B) Rapid rail Howth–Dún Laoghaire and to Blanchardstown, Ronanstown, and Dundrum; busway to Tallaght; diesel train Dún Laoghaire–Bray.

(C) Semi-metro to serve Blanchardstown, Ballymun, Ronanstown, Tallaght, and Leopardstown; diesel train on Howth–Bray.

(D) Diesel train Howth–Bray and to Blanchardstown and Ronanstown; busways to Finglas, Tallaght, and Leopardstown.

The 1989–93 policy decision to serve Tallaght by diesel train on an existing line with a connecting bus service is therefore based on alternative D, with the lowest cost and highest ratio of benefit to cost. The impact on the share of public transport in peak hour traffic in the city centre is likely to be minimal. The main impact of the higher-cost alternative strategies is to move public transport passengers from low-cost to high-cost modes rather than from private to public transport.

THE MARKET FOR RAIL FREIGHT
The rail share of total freight movements in 1988 was 9.8 per cent. In the 1980s the highest share attained by the railways in the freight market was 12.6 per cent, in 1982 (table 50). Barrett

Table 50 Rail freight volumes, 1979–90 (000 tonnes)

COMMODITY	1979 ACTUAL	1979 ADJUSTED*	1985 ACTUAL	TARGET	1989 ACTUAL	1990 TARGET
Cement	807	1,067	580	1,445	645	1,620
Ores	1,026		837	1,290	621	1,200
Petrol, oil	325		62	290	51	300
Beet, pulp	224		179	180	142	180
Ale, beer, stout	203		191	220	168	240
Fertiliser	280	350	285	550	204	580
General	874		1,245	1,120	1,236	1,210
Total	3,739	1,417	3,379	4,933	3,067	5,330

* Adjusted for industrial disputes

Source: CIE Annual Reports; McKinsey Report (1981), 4.3.

(1982, p. 138) estimates that the rail market share was 16.4 per cent in 1970 and 22.4 per cent in 1960.

The decline of 10 per cent in the volume of rail freight between 1980 and 1989 contrasts with the expectation of the McKinsey Report that rail freight volumes would increase by 2 per cent a year. Actual freight volumes in 1985 were 68 per cent of the McKinsey forecast. Volumes in 1989 were 58 per cent of the McKinsey forecast for 1990.

Cement accounted for 53 per cent of the shortfall between the McKinsey target and actual volumes carried in 1985. McKinsey assumed that the loss of volume caused by an industrial dispute in 1979 would be recovered and that rail would increase its market share in the 1990s at the expense of road. In the 1970s cement sales increased by 57 per cent, but the rail share declined from 59 to 40 per cent. By contrast, between 1980 and 1988 there was a decline in cement sales of 43 per cent. Rail carryings of cement also declined by 43 per cent from their adjusted value of 1.067 million tonnes in 1979 to 606,000 tonnes in 1988. It appears therefore that the traffic lost in the industrial dispute has not been recovered and that the new bulk silos built at Cork, Athenry, Sligo, Tullamore and Waterford did not attract extra cement traffic to the railways. Cement sales in 1979 depended on an artificially high investment ratio to GNP, which in turn depended on an unsustainable level of public sector borrowing requirement. The contraction of the market for cement between 1979 and 1988 contrasts with the McKinsey expectations that total sales of cement would grow by a third and that rail would increase its share from 52 to 64 per cent.

Ores accounted for 22 per cent of the shortfall between target and performance of the rail freight sector in 1985. The volume decline was 19 per cent. The closure of mines at Bennetsbridge and Silvermines ended traffic that accounted for 65 per cent of the 1979 ore traffic by rail. Road carryings of ore and metal waste declined by 32 per cent between 1980 and 1988 (Road Freight Transport Survey, 1988, p. 28).

Petrol and oil accounted for 14 per cent of the 1985 rail freight shortfall. 81 per cent of the 1979 volumes was lost by the railways by 1985, and this increased further to 86 per cent by 1988. Road freight tonne-kilometres of petroleum products fell by 10 per cent between 1980 and 1988. Rail's market share therefore declined heavily in the period.

Fertiliser accounted for 16 per cent of the rail freight shortfall between actual and forecast volumes carried in 1985. In the 1970s fertiliser sales increased by 61 per cent, and the rail market share fell from 39 per cent to 17 per cent. McKinsey forecast that the market would grow by 4 per cent per year between 1982 and 1990 and that the rail market share would recover to 30 per cent in 1985. Rail carriage of fertiliser declined by 16 per cent between 1979 and 1988 while the decline in road carriage was 4 per cent.

The rail volumes of **beer, ale and stout** in 1985 were 6 per cent below target. **Beet and pulp** reached its target, while the volumes carried in the **general freight** and other category exceeded the target by 8 per cent.

The 1990 targets for rail freight are unlikely to be met. Shortfalls are likely in the case of cement, because of lower-than-expected sales and a decline in the rail share. Petrol and oil sales are likely to increase, but this traffic has been rapidly lost to other modes. Fertiliser sales are unlikely to rise, because of changes in agricultural policy at EC level, and the rail share is falling. Rail carriage of ores depends on the location of new mines close to the network. Rail volumes of this traffic remained in steady decline between 1985 and 1988. The future of sugar beet carriage by rail is also heavily influenced by EC quotas. The closure of Tuam and Thurles sugar factories, which handled 98 per cent of rail beet in 1979, will reduce rail volumes by transferring beet to factories not usually served by rail. McKinsey found that Carlow had no rail traffic in beet in 1979 and that Mallow handled only 2 per cent of the total.

In 1989 rail freight was only 58 per cent of the 1990 target. Between 1985 and 1989 rail freight volumes declined by 9 per cent. A considerable shortfall is likely therefore between forecast and actual rail freight volumes in 1990, because of the loss of traffic on which McKinsey based its forecasts for the 1980s. Six of the seven major rail freight traffic categories are significantly short of target performance for the 1980s (table 50).

McKinsey (1981, 4.19) found that two-thirds of the **sundries** business was lost by the railways between 1972 and 1979. The remaining rail sundries business lost £6 million on revenues of £3.6 million in 1979. The report notes (4.20) that 'interviews carried out in 1977 by CIE's consultants, Martin and Voorhees, clearly indicated consumer dissatisfaction—all the ex-customers interviewed claimed significant improvements in efficiency at reduced unit cost since they had started using alternative distribution systems.' The alternatives chosen were own-account and private haulier road services.

McKinsey also found that in the unit load sector CIE's domestic volumes declined by 40 per cent between 1978 and 1980 and that there was a loss of 50,000 tonnes of liner train traffic in October 1979, when the B and I Line service was terminated. With RORO gaining at the expense of LOLO in the foreign trade sector, railways were losing a potential market in Ireland's large foreign trade sector. RORO increased from 36 per cent of LOLO in 1975 to equality in 1980.

The decline in rail freight in the 1980s reflects the decline of industries such as cement and mining. The decline in volume of fertiliser carried by rail reflects changed EC policies on agriculture, while petrol and oil transport was changed to road and coastal shipping. The earlier declines in sundries and container traffic by rail reflect changes in distribution patterns and the growth of RORO port traffic.

Table 51			
Commodity composition of rail freight shortfall in 1985 and proportion of 1990 target attained in 1989			
COMMODITY	1985 SHORTFALL (TONNES)	%	1989 AS SHARE OF 1990 TARGET (%)
Cement	865	53	40
Ores	453	22	52
Beet, pulp	1	0	79
Petrol, oil	228	14	17
Ale, beer, stout	29	2	70
Fertiliser	265	16	35
General	(125)*	(8)*	102
Total	1626	100	58

* ( ) indicates surplus over target

Source: CIE annual reports; McKinsey Report (1981).

Industrial output increased by 90 per cent in volume between 1980 and 1989. The volume of Irish exports increased by 103 per cent in the same period, while the volume of retail sales fell by 5 per cent. The depressed home market is reflected in the growth of only 12 per cent in the output of the traditional manufacturing industries between 1980 and 1989. In the same period the output of the modern manufacturing sector rose from an index of 100 to 401. The railways relied heavily on six major categories of traffic, and suffered both from stagnation in these industries and loss of market share to roads. By contrast the new manufacturers concentrated on the export markets. Road hauliers and own-account operators increased their foreign tonne-kilometres by 86 per cent between 1980 and 1988. The changing structure of the economy has reduced the railway share of freight steadily, and this is likely to continue in the future.

Table 52			
Northern Ireland and overseas haulage by Republic of Ireland firms, 1980–88 (million tonne-kilometres)			
MARKET	1980	1988	INDEX
Northern Ireland	62.6	85.7	137
Overseas	271.8	535.5	197
Total export haulage	334.4	621.2	186

Source: Central Statistics Office, Road Freight Transport Surveys.

CIE BUS SERVICES
In 1989 CIE bus services had customer receipts of £152 million, or 2.11 times its railway customer receipts. Table 53 shows the main features of CIE bus operations between 1980 and 1989 for the four bus sectors: Dublin, other cities, provincial, and tours.

The operating ratio for the combined services increased from 76 to 88 per cent. This improvement reduced the 1989 deficit by

Table 53

CIE bus service results, 1980–89

(1) DUBLIN	1980	1989	INDEX
Passengers (million)	175.1	161.2	92
Receipts (£ million)	35.0	74.9	214
Expenditure (£ million)	51.6	90.7	176
Deficit (£ million)	16.6	15.8	95
Operating ratio (%)	68	83	121
(2) OTHER CITIES			
Passengers (million)	23.7	19.8	84
Receipts (£ million)	4.8	9.5	198
Expenditure (£ million)	8.1	12.0	148
Deficit (£ million)	3.2	2.5	78
Operating ratio (%)	59	79	134
(3) PROVINCIAL			
Passengers (million)	46.5	43.5	94
Receipts (£ million)	26.6	64.4	242
Expenditure (£ million)	27.6	65.9	239
Deficit (£ million)	1.0	1.5	150
Operating ratio (%)	96	94	98
(4) TOURS			
Passengers (million)	2.0	0.1	5
Receipts (£ million)	3.0	2.7	90
Expenditure (£ million)	3.7	3.7	100
Deficit (£ million)	0.7	1.0	143
Operating ratio (%)	81	73	90
TOTAL			
Passengers (million)	247.3	224.6	91
Receipts (£ million)	69.4	151.5	218
Expenditure (£ million)	91.0	172.3	189
Deficit (£ million)	21.6	20.8	96
Operating ratio (%)	76	88	116

Note: Day tours and private hire were included in the 'Tours' category up to 1985, when they were transferred to the 'Provincial' category.

Source: CIE Annual Reports.

£20.7 million. The improvement in the operating ratio occurred because the increase in real revenues was greater than the increase in real expenditure. Despite a 9 per cent decline in passenger numbers, receipts in 1989 were 218 per cent of those in 1980 while expenditure was 189 per cent greater. Consumer prices rose by 103 per cent between 1980 and 1989.

Real fares per passenger therefore increased by 16 per cent between 1980 and 1989. Real expenditure rose by 3 per cent per passenger. The real deficit per passenger declined by 7 per cent. While progress was made in reducing the deficit from 24 per cent to 12 per cent of the cost of bus services in the period 1980–89, the improvement occurred because a smaller number of passengers paid substantially higher fares. This strategy may not be as successful if the Government implements its decision to deregulate the market for bus services.

The analysis of the increase in real revenues and costs per passenger shows that in Dublin fares rose by 12 per cent while costs fell by 12 per cent. In the provincial cities costs were reduced by 8 per cent while fares rose by 11 per cent. On the provincial services costs per passenger rose by 34 per cent while fares rose 31 per cent. Part of the cost and revenue escalation may be due to changes in journey length; but the bus passenger-miles series was withdrawn from the CIE Annual Report after 1969. The output of CIE bus services, measured in vehicle-kilometres, fell between 1980 and 1989 by 3 per cent; the real cost per vehicle-kilometre therefore increased by 6 per cent.

Bus services in Dublin and the other cities face difficult operating conditions because of the lack of a mechanism to ration urban road space efficiently. The tendency towards low-density suburbs creates problems for public transport also in Irish cities. In Dublin the use of the bus service peaked in 1965, when there were 248 million passengers. By 1979 the passenger numbers had declined to 167 million. The Transport Consultative Commission pointed out that the decline in number of fare-paying passengers in the 1970s was even more dramatic than the loss of 42 million in total passenger numbers between 1970/71 and 1979. There were 61 million fewer fare-paying passengers on the Dublin Bus service in 1979 than in 1970/71. This was a loss of 31 per cent of fare-paying passengers. The number availing of free travel schemes increased two-and-a-half times, from 12.5 million to 31.9 million; without the free travel scheme the Dublin city bus service in 1979 would have had only 54 per cent of the passengers it carried in 1965 (Transport Consultative Commission, 1980, p. 99).

Passenger numbers on the provincial city services also declined during the 1970s, from 42 million in 1970 to 24 million in 1980, a fall of 43 per cent. It is also likely that the decline in number of fare-paying passengers was greater in this sector than the decline in total passenger numbers. In a study of the use of concessionary travel passes in Galway, Loughrea, and Clifden, O'Mahony (1986) found that 48 per cent of those interviewed in Galway city used the pass once or more a week, compared with 2 per cent in Loughrea rural district and no use at all in the Clifden rural district.

The school bus service has been included in the accounts of the CIE provincial bus sector. Thus McKinsey (1981, p. 9) reported that the sector's apparent improvement in the late 1960s 'in both revenue and profits has been largely due to the introduction of the school bus programme.' In 1989 the revenue was £64.4 million, which included £32.0 million from school transport. More than half the revenue of this sector is now based on the school contract, which is not open for competitive tendering directly to the Department of Education. CIE subcontracts some 60 per cent of the service to private operators (Annual Report, 1987, p. 5); this will have to be addressed in the context of overall deregulation of bus services. Even if CIE were to retain its monopoly on tendering for the service and to resist Government attempts to reduce the cost, the revenue from the service will fall because of the decline in the population of school-going age. This is predicted to fall from 1,031,800 to 809,200 between 1986 and 2001 (CSO Labour Force and Population Projections, 1991–2021, 1988).

CIE'S OTHER BUSINESSES

The road freight sector made a profit of £0.5 million in 1989 and had an operative ratio of 103 per cent. By contrast, the operating ratio in 1983 was 93 per cent.

Table 54 shows the adjustments made in CIE road freight during the 1980s in returning the sector to the profitability it had shown in the 1950s and 1960s. In the years 1980–89 CIE road freight receipts rose 22 per cent and costs 6 per cent, compared with a rise in the consumer price index of 103 per cent. The vehicle fleet was halved, and the share of the receipts accounted for by CIE's own vehicles was reduced from 87 to 66 per cent, indicating the greater use of contractors' vehicles. The company share of the national market was allowed to fall. The road freight business was deregulated in September 1988, with entry open to all who meet the quality controls of the Road Transport Act, 1986. CIE's position in the market is small but profitable. At the end of 1989 its fleet had only 23 per cent of the number of vehicles in 1971/72. Northern Ireland Carriers, in many ways the counterpart of CIE road freight, shrank to about one-third of its original staff and vehicle fleet between the liberalisation of the Northern Ireland internal market in 1965 and 1984 (Campbell, 1984).

Rosslare Harbour returned a profit of £1.8 million on receipts of £4.8 million in 1989, compared with a profit of £0.5 million on receipts of £1.9 million in 1980. Rosslare increased its share of Irish exports and imports by value from 1 per cent in 1964 to 11.4 per cent in 1984 (Green Paper, 1985, p. 52). In 1989 Rosslare was the largest port for accompanied cars and buses, with 43 per cent of the total. It had 27 per cent of RORO freight.

ARAN ISLANDS FERRY SERVICE
Customer receipts from the Aran Islands service in 1980 were £0.2 million, a deficit of £0.3 million, while costs were £0.5 million. The revenue-to-cost ratio was 40 per cent; by 1989 it had declined to 24 per cent.

The CIE Annual Report for 1987 (p. 10) stated that customer receipts decreased again 'and are now 65% below 1981 levels.' The 1989 receipts declined a further 21 per cent, to £140,000. This was 24 per cent of the expenditure on the service of £578,000.

The CIE vessel *Naomh Éanna* has been withdrawn from the service, which is now provided by a chartered freight vessel and privately owned passenger ferries under contract. Since CIE's financial difficulties are accounted for by the erosion of the company's market share by private operators in the years 1980 to 1987 rather than cost escalation within the company, it is ironic that it is now providing a subsidy from public funds to the private sector for the carriage of passengers between Galway and Aran. The case for subsidy in this market needs clarification. The CIE Annual Report for 1988 stated that 'substantial investment will be required if the Company is requested to provide a Roll-on/Roll-off ferry service to the Island'; the 1989 Annual Report stated that 'the service was provided during 1989 by chartered freight vessels and contracted privately owned ferries.'

CATERING SERVICES
This sector had an operating ratio of 104 per cent in 1989, with a profit of £0.2 million on revenues of £4.7 million. In 1980 this sector had a loss of £0.3 million and revenues of £7.8 million. The sector then included the Great Southern Hotels, which were transferred to the Minister for Labour in March 1984 with accumulated losses of £9.85 million. The remaining catering services, on trains and at stations and depots, recorded losses of

£0.35 million in 1984 and £0.16 million in 1985. Profits of £47,000 were recorded in 1986, £105,000 in 1987, and £179,000 in 1988.

CANALS
The canal system had costs of £1 million in 1980 and revenues of only £40,250. In July 1986 responsibility for the canals was transferred to the Office of Public Works. In 1985, their last full year in the CIE accounts, the canals had receipts of £56,000 and expenditure of £1.44 million.

CONSULTANCY
The company's consultancy business, CIE Consult, was established in April 1987 and markets transport management and engineering services in Ireland and abroad. It incurred a small loss in 1987; in 1988 a loss of £55,000 was incurred on incomes of £865,000. In 1989 the loss was £173,000 on a revenue of £356,000.

THE CIE TARGETS, 1983–88
In 1983 the Government decided 'as an interim measure' to introduce a formula related to CIE's revenues and expenditure as a basis for settling the annual subvention. It was decided to pay the company a subsidy of half its revenues or one-third of its costs, whichever was the lower. The 1983 policy also set cost reduction targets for CIE as a whole and for the railways. The company was required to reduce its annual expenditure in real terms by 12 per cent over a five-year period, with 1983 as the base year. In the case of the railways the target was to reduce overall rail costs by close to a fifth over five years (Comprehensive Public Expenditure Programmes, 1985, p. 207; Green Paper, 1985, p. 12).

In 1983 total CIE expenditure was £294 million. The target therefore required a reduction of £35 million in expenditure at 1983 prices, to £259 million. This is the equivalent of £324 million at 1988 prices when adjusted by the increase in the consumer price index of 25 per cent between 1983 and 1988. Actual expenditure by CIE in 1988 was £346 million; this was 6.7 per cent above the target set by the Government.

The railway target was to 'reduce overall rail costs by close to one-fifth over five years.' The costs of the railway in 1983, updated to 1988, are shown in table 55. The target for rail expenditure

Table 55	**Railway costs, 1983 and 1988 (£ million)**				
	COSTS IN 1983	AT 1988 PRICES	1988 TARGET	1988 ACTUAL	EXCESS
Mainline	119.2	149.0	119.2	124.1	4.9
Howth–Bray	8.1	10.1	8.1	25.4	17.5
Total	127.3	159.1	127.3	149.5	22.2

Source: CIE annual reports.

was exceeded by £4.9 million on mainline rail and £22.2 million for the system as a whole.

Railway costs in 1988 were 15 per cent greater than the target set in 1983. Progress on the cost reduction programme was not analysed in the Annual Reports, and there was no review when the five-year programme ended in 1988.

The railway accounts show expenditure under seven categories. Table 56 shows these categories as a proportion of total railway costs in 1983 and the real growth of each category between 1983 and 1988; it can be seen that fuel and renewal of lines and works exceeded the cost reduction target and that there was a below-target reduction on maintenance of lines and works. On the other hand there were real increases in financial charges and in operating depreciation. The maintenance of rolling stock cost 22 per cent more than the target, chiefly because of an increase in the mainline sector. The large category 'Operating and other expenses' accounted for 46 per cent of total costs in the base year and was 21 per cent greater than target in 1988.

RAILWAY PRODUCTIVITY

The outputs of freight and passenger units by eleven major EC railway companies in 1986 are shown in table 57. Taking the Irish output of 253.7 traffic units per staff member as 100, the average for the eleven railway systems combined has an index of 144. Irish railway productivity was 69 per cent of the average for the eleven systems combined. To have attained the productivity of the combined system, Irish railways would have required a staff of 4,500 in 1986, some 2,000 fewer than actually employed.

By 1989, staff numbers on the Irish railways had declined to 5,889, but the railways were still overmanned by 31 per cent compared with the EC productivity standards of three years earlier. Staff costs on CIE rail in 1989 were £94.8 million, so that the cost of overmanning by EC standards was £29.4 million.

Table 56		
Growth of railway costs during cost reduction programme		
Cost category	Proportion of costs (%)	1988 cost index (1983 = 100)
Maintenance of lines and works	14	88
Maintenance of rolling stock	15	102
Fuel	7	61
Operating and other expenses	45	101
Renewal of lines and works	8	69
Operating depreciation	5	138
Financial charges	6	206
Total	100	101*
* Target index: 80		

This would have reduced total railway costs to £124.1 million in 1989 and eliminated over four-fifths of the gap between actual and target expenditure. The operating ratio would have increased from 47 to 58 per cent. The operating ratio declined slightly from 48 to 47 per cent in the 1980s; in the 1970s the ratio was 79 per cent (McKinsey Report, 1981, p. A11).

Table 57

Railway productivity in EC countries, 1986

	PASSENGER KM (000)	FREIGHT KM (000)	STAFF (000)	TRAFFIC UNITS PER STAFF	INDEX
Ireland	1,075	574	6.5	253.7	100
Belgium	6,069	7,442	54.9	246.1	97
Denmark	4,536	1,791	21.4	295.7	116
France	59,862	51,690	233.4	477.9	188
Germany	41,397	59,630	257.0	393.1	155
Greece	1,950	702	14.6	181.6	72
Italy	40,500	17,410	214.8	269.6	106
Netherlands	8,919	3,107	27.9	431.0	170
Portugal	5,803	1,448	23.0	315.3	124
Spain	6,363	18,552	66.3	375.9	148
UK	30,800	18,153	142.7	343.0	135
	207,395	180,488	1,062.9	364.9	144

Source: European Conference of Ministers of Transport, *Statistical Trends in Transport, 1965–86.*

THE EVOLUTION OF TRANSPORT POLICY

Issues such as contestability, social cost, value for money and adaptation to the EC internal market are likely to dominate transport policy in the future.

The development of contestability theory by William Baumol and Elizabeth Bailey, culminating in the United States in the Airline Deregulation Act of 1978 and Baumol's presidential address to the American Economics Association in 1981, struck a serious blow against regulatory policies designed to prevent market entry. The crucial role of new market entrants in ensuring the efficiency of established firms was illustrated in a series of airline, bus and haulage deregulations.

As the deregulated market matured, however, it became a cause for concern that established companies erected new barriers to contestability to replace their use of 'regulatory capture', or had governments deter new entrants on their behalf. The work of Bailey and Williams, Levine and Kahn illustrates this phase in the United States. While Ireland derived massive benefits from deregulating its principal market between Ireland and Britain, Europe as a whole is becoming oligopolistic without having experienced the benefits of deregulation. The substantial barriers to new entrants in European aviation and the reluctance of existing national airlines to cease over four decades of price collusion mean that European deregulation in 1993 may meet Richard Pryke's forecast of 'a monopolistic damp squib'. On the other hand, policies to deal with new market entry, price collusion, predatory pricing, hub airport dominance, abuse of dominant position and information bias in computer reservation systems could generate in Europe the significant gains from airline deregulation in Ireland. Policies to eliminate economic rents in a deregulated European aviation sector must therefore be a priority.

In late 1990 the obstacles to the operation of new airlines in Europe are so great that market entry is unlikely. The basic assumption underlying contestable markets—ease of entry—is not met. The industry is unlikely to attract new entrants unless the obstacles to competition are removed.

The allocation of slots at busy airports is at present controlled by the 'grandfather rights' system. The Draft Code of Conduct for Slot Allocation prepared by the EC Transport Directorate proposes a special category of new-entrant status. The slot co-ordinator would be required to ensure that new airlines would receive slots to introduce a new service up to a maximum of the number of services operated at present but not more than two slots per four-hour period.

Predatory pricing is now controlled in the EC by two limitations. The first requires a special examination of fare increases of more than 20 per cent, and the second gives airlines or states the right to appeal to the Commission to decide whether a proposed increase meets defined criteria for automatic acceptance. A system of double disapproval, in which fares may be charged unless they are refused by both states served, will be introduced in 1993.

Under the June 1990 package of liberalisation measures agreed by the EC Council of Transport Ministers, three zones of fare flexibility are now in operation. Within these zones fares are automatically allowed without government approval. In the business fare category a variation of plus or minus 5 per cent is allowed with automatic approval. For promotional business rates the fare charged may vary between 94 and 80 per cent of the business fare with automatic approval. Tourist promotional fares may range between 30 and 79 per cent of the business fare with automatic approval.

The exemptions under article 85.3 for ground handling monopolies and computer reservation systems also expire in January 1991. The EC Code of Conduct for CRS has removed a potential barrier to the contestability of aviation in Europe. Choice of a number of suppliers of ground handling services would remove a source of economic rent from the airlines that have this right at present. The main obstacles to a contestable aviation sector in Europe are, however, lack of slot access at hub airports and the risk of retaliatory price responses by incumbents to new entrants.

The threshold for multiple designation was lowered from 140,000 passengers a year after November 1990 to 100,000 a year after January 1992. Multiple designation increases contestability. The report on the first year of implementation of the December 1987 policy (EC, 1989, p. 10) found that 'the number

6

of routes where more than one carrier of one Member State has operated has increased from 22 in 1987 to 33 in 1989. On the other hand it should be noted that only five Member States have given their airlines the benefit of multiple designation. Furthermore, it should be noted that the airlines designated by a Member State cannot always act independently. It is remarkable that many of the routes with multiple designation are routes which do not meet the thresholds set out in the decision and that these same Member States were hesitant to allow their airlines to compete on the busy routes.'

The contestability of European aviation might also be increased by competition between the existing national airlines. Price competition has not yet occurred between these airlines, but capacity competition has been permitted. The traditional 50/50 market sharing was replaced by 55/45 in 1988 and 60/40 in 1989. Market shares may change by 7.5 per cent per year up to 1992, giving a possible 75/25 market split. There will be no safety net after 1 January 1993 for the weaker carrier.

Fifth-freedom services allow an airline on an international service to a foreign country to pick up and set down passengers in another country. Aer Lingus, for example, has developed traffic from Manchester to Amsterdam, Paris, Zürich, Milan, Copenhagen, and Hamburg. Price initiatives by carriers providing these services are not allowed. The limitation on these services was 30 per cent of the seats provided; in December 1989 the Council of Transport Ministers decided to allow 50 per cent of seats on these flights to be sold to fifth-freedom passengers and to allow price leadership by fifth-freedom carriers.

There are no agreements on cabotage within the EC. The Commission proposed in July 1989 that 30 per cent of the seats on, for example, Nice–London could be sold between Nice and Paris.

The deregulated European market after 1 January 1993 may either be highly contestable or show little change from the present, with the most expensive unrestricted fares in the world. If new entrants are excluded by obstacles such as hub airport dominance and predatory pricing, and existing national carriers are permitted to acquire the smaller carriers and continue to share European markets, the consumer interest may have to be served by opening Europe's markets to outside carriers from areas such as North America and the Asia-Pacific region.

Given the dominance of Irish aviation by Irish airlines, the contestability of aviation here requires continuation of the two-airline policy adopted in September 1989. O'Mahony (1988) described the roles of the two airlines in stimulating the total Irish aviation market as follows: 'Ryanair proved to be a catalyst in introducing the concept of low air fares to Ireland... Aer Lingus have shown remarkable vigour in their response to the new competitive environment.' In a fully contestable EC aviation market, airlines from other countries could have an impact similar to that of Ryanair. However, the many anti-competitive developments in European aviation in recent years indicate that the two-airline policy remains necessary. The 1989 policy allocated the London hubs at Heathrow and Gatwick to Aer Lingus and at Luton and Stansted to Ryanair. The Munich route and the direct services from regional airports were allocated to Ryanair, with regional services through the Dublin hub to be developed by Aer Lingus.

In implementing bus deregulation in Ireland the contestability of the market requires controlling the dominant position of both Dublin Bus and Bus Éireann. The experience in Britain shows that new entrants faced predation in the period 1980–83. The contestability of the British bus sector was subsequently improved by privatisation, which imposed a bankruptcy constraint on the National Bus Company, and by splitting the NBC into seventy-two separate companies to prevent market dominance. Neither of these measures is likely in Ireland; administrative measures to promote contestability and deal with predation pricing will therefore be required.

In England 85 per cent of bus routes were found to be commercial after bus deregulation and 15 per cent required subsidy through a system of public tendering. This implements the prescription of Demsetz (1967) that competition *for* a market should apply when competition *in* the market is not possible. In Anglo-Irish airline deregulation no application of Demsetz was required after deregulation: while cross-subsidisation of thin routes from the Dublin–London route had been part of the case for preventing competition, deregulation resulted both in significant fare reductions on trunk routes and an unprecedented growth of regional services.

The remaining areas of regulation in Irish transport that are likely to be reassessed in an era of deregulation include the taxi service and the requirement that North American air services stop at Shannon.

In 1990 the Davy Kelleher McCarthy report on the Shannon stop-over stated that the policy caused delay costs and diversion of traffic via London, and prevented the development of Dublin as a hub. Since Dublin's short-haul traffic is nine times that of Shannon, it is able to support a wider range of feeder services as centre of a hub-and-spoke system. In a deregulated market Shannon would have a daily New York service, and Dublin would develop direct services, drawing traffic from Northern Ireland and British regional airports, its feeder services on twenty-five routes, and recovering traffic lost to Heathrow.

The Envision report, on the other hand, stressed the benefits of Shannon to the mid-west region. It found approval for the stop-over among tourist passengers using the service and among travel agents. Advantages such as US immigration control at Shannon and the airport's lack of congestion were stressed, and its 61 per cent market share of North American route passengers in 1988.

Shannon's North American route traffic in 1990 was split between Aer Lingus (90 per cent) and Delta (10 per cent). Since airlines are the customers of airports, it is necessary for Shannon to attract more carriers. The Atlantic Express project involves a Shannon hub connecting North American services with regional services to twelve British provincial cities, thereby avoiding congestion and poor regional connections at Heathrow and Gatwick. The project requires a joint venture between North American carriers and smaller European carriers interlining at a Shannon hub.

As emphasis in public policy moves from preventing competition on behalf of existing companies to promoting it on behalf of consumers and new entrants to the market, the state will have to address matters of social cost. Preventing competition, subsidising deficits and nationalising enterprises do not reduce social cost.

Social costs and property rights should be examined in the light of Coase's theorem (Coase, 1960). The established airlines' property rights to major airport space, to the exclusion of new entrants, is an obvious inefficiency, as is the exclusive property right of the military to large sections of European air-space. Coase makes the case for allowing compensation and exchange in the efficient solution of the problem. In transport, social costs are assumed to be infinite in cases such as bans on night flying at airports and restrictions on the expansion of Heathrow and Gatwick. This veto could be replaced with mechanisms by which the gainers could compensate the losers, leaving both parties better off.

The social cost of urban motoring has been seen to be substantial, but few mechanisms, apart from congestion, exist to control this social cost. Pricing and/or controls on urban motoring are likely to be introduced as the investment cost and social cost of urban motoring become unacceptable.

The social benefits of rail travel are assumed to be greater than the private benefits, albeit without supporting evidence. Nonetheless the users pay less than half the cost. The accounts of CIE were restructured in 1990 to give transparency to the level of state support, following a direction from the Government.

The third major theme in the evolution of Irish transport policy in the 1990s is likely to be value for money in public expenditure. The era of deficit finance is set to end, and reductions in the debt/GNP ratio and high tax rates are likely to curb any revival of public expenditure growth. The large infrastructure investments in transport will be assessed from the point of view of value for money, as will the public transport subsidy.

The recovery in the economy after 1987 was accomplished under a policy of reducing the exchequer borrowing requirement from 12.8 per cent of GNP in 1986 to 2.1 per cent in 1990. The public capital programme was reduced from a volume index of 128 in 1982 to 100 in 1985 and 70 in 1989.

McAleese (1990) states that 'the standard Keynesian-type model would predict that a fiscal contraction, by withdrawing purchasing power from the economy, would depress consumption and investment and adversely affect GDP. The evidence shows that fiscal adjustment, far from weakening the growth process, may be essential to its continuance. Irish GNP grew by less than 1% in the period 1980–86 compared with 3.7% per annum 1987–89.'

The period after 1987 was therefore one of 'expansionary fiscal contraction', in which the expansion of the economy coincided with the contraction of Government borrowing and the reduction of income tax rates. Despite the success of expansionary fiscal contraction Ireland has strong public expenditure lobbies, including several in transport.

Adaptation of the transport sector to the internal EC market requires a three-pronged approach, according to a report prepared for the Europen Bureau of the Department of the Taoiseach (Crowley, 1990). Ireland should seek recognition of, and financial assistance for, its problems of peripherality, size, and poor infrastructure. It should rapidly liberalise its transport sector and promote the awareness of Irish business generally of the opportunities presented by the single market.

The areas of opportunity include the abolition of frontier controls, the right of cabotage or the operation of transport services within other states, reductions in vehicle cost disadvantages due to tax harmonisation, and the opening of the Channel Tunnel.

The Europen Report cites average costs of border formalities per consignment in intra-EC trade, ranging from 26 ECU per consignment in Belgium to 130 ECU in Italy. The Chartered Institute of Transport (1987) estimated that the road haulage industry had a cost disadvantage of 16 per cent compared with Northern Ireland hauliers. About two-thirds of this cost disadvantage was caused by VAT, fuel, vehicle price and interest charge differences. These should converge in the internal market. The remaining source of cost disadvantage was the higher wages paid by road hauliers in the Republic.

Ferris (1990) finds that the Channel Tunnel can have a positive impact on Ireland's freight and passenger movements to the Continent, in the form of reduced journey times and transport costs and ease of delivering goods. The Channel Tunnel is likely to bring 'substantially lower prices for passengers and freight', but 'the extent of the positive impact on Ireland is dependent on the quality of road and rail links between the Tunnel and west British ports.' Ferris forecasts that 'the real growth of freight traffic through Britain is likely to take place in unaccompanied freight traffic i.e. lift-on/lift-off container traffic and unaccompanied roll-on/roll-off freight, travelling through Britain to the Channel Tunnel by train.' There may also be some re-routing to the tunnel of freight from Ireland's direct sea services to the Continent, and the direct routes may also lose market share in car passengers. Ferris forecasts some growth in rail passenger numbers, 'but only if attractive rail packages can be devised, with good rail services that have the minimum of inter-rail connecting in Britain.' However, it is unlikely that the surface modes can be successful in competition with the low holiday air fares and the large time savings enjoyed by air passengers over the surface modes between Ireland and the Continent.

The pressures of the internal market will dictate the dominant themes in Irish transport policy in the 1990s. These are likely to include the minimisation of commercial, social and taxpayer costs of the transport sector with the emphasis on promoting contestability in the market and the control of social costs.

NOTES

1. THE REGULATION OF AVIATION

Airports Policy (Cmnd 9542), London: HMSO 1984.

Bailey, Elizabeth, and Williams, J., 'Sources of rent in the deregulated airline industry', *Journal of Law and Economics*, vol. 31 (1988), 173–202.

Barrett, Seán D., *Airports for Sale: the Case for Competition*, London: Adam Smith Institute 1984.

—*Flying High: Airline Price and European Regulation*, Aldershot: Gower 1987.

—'Europe's congested airspace: time for market solutions', *Economic Affairs*, June 1989.

Baumol, William J., 'Contestable markets: an uprising in the theory of industrial structure', *American Economic Review*, vol. 72 (1982), 1–15.

Civil Aviation Authority, *Air Traffic Distribution in the London Area: a Consultative Document* (CAA Paper 510), London 1985.

—*Air Traffic Distribution in the London Area: Advice to the Secretary of State* (CAA Paper 522), London 1986.

—*Competition on the Main Domestic Trunk Routes* (CAA Paper 87005), London 1987.

Coase, R., 'The problem of social cost', *Journal of Law and Economics*, vol. 3 (1960).

Demsetz, H., 'Towards a theory of property rights', *American Economic Review*, vol. 57 (1967).

Doganis, R., *Flying Off Course: the Economics of International Airlines*, London: Unwin 1985.

Economist Intelligence Unit, *Travel and Tourism in the Single European Market*, London 1989.

European Civil Aviation Conference, *Report of the Task Force on Competition in Intra-European Air Services* [the Compass Report], Paris 1981.

European Community, *Air Transport: a Community Approach*, 1979.

—*Report on Regional Air Services*, 1980.

—*Report on Scheduled Passenger Air Fares in the EC* [includes the 'Cascade Studies'], 1981.

—*Civil Aviation Memorandum No. 2*, 1984.

—*Directives on Fares for Scheduled Aviation, Market Access, Capacity Sharing and Competition* (*Official Journal*, L374, 31 December 1987).

—*Report on the First Year* [1988] *of the Implementation of the Aviation Policy Approved in December 1987* (COM 89.476), 1989.

—*Reports on Competition Policy* (annual).

International Civil Aviation Organisation, *Surveys of International Air Transport Fares and Rates*, Montreal (annual).

Jordan, W., *Airline Regulation in America*, Baltimore: Johns Hopkins University Press 1970.

Kahn, A., 'Surprises of airline deregulation', *American Economic Review*, vol. 78 (1988), 312–22.

Levine, M., 'Airline competition in deregulated markets: theory, firm strategy and public policy', *Yale Journal on Regulation*, vol. 4 (1987), 393–494.

Monopolies and Mergers Commission, *The British Airports Authority* (Cmnd 9644), London: HMSO 1985.

National Consumer Council, *Air Transport and the Consumer*, London: HMSO 1986.

Organisation for Economic Co-operation and Development, *Deregulation and Airline Competition*, Paris 1988.

Pryke, Richard, 'American Deregulation and European Liberalisation', ESRC Seminar, Oxford, 1989.

2. PORTS AND SHIPPING

B and I Line, Annual Report, Dublin 1989.

Comprehensive Public Expenditure Programmes, 1988, Dublin: Stationery Office 1989.

Dublin Chamber of Commerce, *Corridor to Competitiveness,* Dublin 1990.

Dublin Docks Review Group [chairman: John M. Horgan], *Report,* Dublin: Labour Court 1984.

National Development Plan, 1989–1993, Dublin: Stationery Office 1989.

3. ROAD INVESTMENT

Advisory Committee on Trunk Road Assessment, *Report* [the Leitch Report], London: HMSO 1977.

Barrett, Seán D., *Transport Policy in Ireland,* Dublin: Irish Management Institute 1982.

Barrett, Seán D., and Walsh, Brendan, 'The user pays principle: theory and applications', in John Blackwell and Frank Convery (eds.), *Promise and Performance: Irish Environmental Policies Analysed,* Dublin: University College Resource and Environmental Policy Centre, 1983.

Bradley, J., and FitzGerald, J., *Medium Term Review, 1989–1994,* Dublin: Economic and Social Research Institute 1989.

European Conference of Ministers of Transport, Annual Report, Paris 1987.

Feeney, B., and Hynes, C., *A Survey of Car Ownership and Use, 1982,* Dublin: An Foras Forbartha 1985.

Gwilliam, K., and Mackie, P. J., *Economics and Transport Policy,* London: Unwin 1975.

Hirschman, A., *The Strategy of Economic Development,* New Haven: Yale University Press 1958.

House of Commons, *Sixth Report from the Estimates Committee, 1968–1969: Motorways and Trunk Roads* (HCP 102-IX), London: HMSO 1969.

Kildare County Council, *Kilcullen Link Environmental Impact Study; Kilcullen Link Noise Analysis Report; Kilcullen Link Areas of Scientific Interest,* Naas 1988.

National Development Plan, 1989–1993 (Pl. 6342), Dublin: Stationery Office 1989.

Road Development, Ireland, 1989 to 1993, Dublin: Stationery Office 1989.

Road Pricing: the Technical and Economic Possibilities [the Smeed Report], London: HMSO 1964.

Sharp, C., *Transport Economics*, London: Macmillan 1973.

4. THE REGULATION OF ROAD TRANSPORT

Balcombe, R. J., Hopkins, J. M., and Penet, K., *Bus Deregulation in Great Britain: a Review of the First Year* (Research Report 161), Crowthorne (Berkshire): Transport and Road Research Laboratory 1988, 23.

Barrett, Seán D., and McLoughlin, D., 'Taxi sharing: Belfast-Leeds-London', *Economic Affairs*, October–December 1984.

Beesley, M., 'The Role of Government in a Deregulated Market (Access, Competition, Safety)', ECMT Round Table 83, Paris 1989.

Buses (Cmnd 9300), London: HMSO 1984.

Conlon, P., Presidential Address, Chartered Institute of Transport, Dublin 1988.

Conroy, J., *A History of Railways in Ireland*, London: Longman / Green 1928.

European Conference of Ministers of Transport, *Regulatory Reform in the Transport Sector*, Paris: ECMT 1987.

Jaffer, S., and Thompson, D., 'Deregulating express coaches: a reassessment', *Fiscal Studies*, November 1986.

Monopolies and Mergers Commission, *Badgerline Holdings and Midland Red West Holdings* (CM 595), London: HMSO 1989.

National Prices Commission, *Study of Taxi and Hackney Services* (Occasional Paper 24), Dublin: National Prices Commission 1977.

Report on Internal Public Transport [the Beddy Report], Dublin: Stationery Office 1957.

Report on Internal Public Transport [the Pacemaker Report], Dublin: CIE 1963.

Report of the Transport Consultative Commission on Road Freight Haulage, Dublin: Stationery Office 1981.

Report of the Tribunal on Public Transport, Dublin: Stationery Office 1939.

Report on Transport in Ireland [the Milne Report], Dublin: Stationery Office 1948.

Robinson, D., 'Bus industry review', *Transport*, September 1989.

Shields, B. F., 'An analysis of the legislation, published accounts, and operating subsidies of the Great Southern Railways Company, 1924–1937', *Journal of the Statistical and Social Inquiry Society of Ireland*, 1937.

Transport Policy: a Green Paper (Pl. 3580), Dublin: Stationery Office 1985.

Vickers, John, and Yarrow, George, *Privatization: an Economic Analysis*, Cambridge (Massachusetts): MIT Press 1988.

5. THE PERFORMANCE OF PUBLIC TRANSPORT

Barrett, Seán D., *Transport Policy in Ireland*, Dublin: Irish Management Institute 1982.

Campbell, B., 'Privatisation: good news or bad?', Chartered Institute of Transport Conference, Dublin, May 1984.

Conlon, P., Presidential Address, Chartered Institute of Transport, Dublin 1988.

O'Mahony, A., *The Elderly in the Community: Transport and Access to Services in Rural Areas*, Dublin: National Council for the Aged 1986.

The Transport Challenge: a Report for the Minister for Transport by McKinsey International Inc., Dublin: Stationery Office 1981.

Transport Consultative Commission, *Report on Passenger Transport Services in the Dublin Area*, Dublin: Stationery Office 1980.

Transport Policy: a Green Paper (Pl. 3580), Dublin: Stationery Office 1985.

6. THE EVOLUTION OF TRANSPORT POLICY

Bailey, Elizabeth, 'Price and productivity change following deregulation: the US experience', *Economic Journal*, vol. 96 (1986), no. 381, 1–17.

Bailey, Elizabeth, and Williams, J., 'Sources of rent in the deregulated airline industry', *Journal of Law and Economics*, vol. 31 (1988), 173–202.

Baumol, William J., 'Contestable markets: an uprising in the theory of industrial structure', *American Economic Review*, vol. 72 (1982), 1–15.

Chartered Institute of Transport, *The Irish Road Haulage Industry: a Study of Competitiveness*, Dublin: CIT 1987.

Coase, R., 'The problem of social cost', *Journal of Law and Economics*, vol. 3 (1960).

Crowley, J., '1992 and the Transport Sector', Dublin: Europen Bureau, Department of the Taoiseach 1990.

Davy Kelleher McCarthy, 'The Shannon Stopover Policy', Dublin. (For the impact on the Shannon region see 'Shannon's Gateway Status: an Analysis', Envision Marketing Consultants, Galway, 1990.)

Demsetz, H., 'Towards a theory of property rights', *American Economic Review*, vol. 57 (1967).

Demsetz, H., 'Why regulate utilities?', *Journal of Law and Economics*, vol. 11 (1968), 55–65.

Ferris, T., 'Transport', *The Single European Market and the Irish Economy*, Dublin: Institute of Public Administration 1990, 186–213.

Kahn, A., *The Economics of Regulation*, Cambridge (Massachusetts): MIT Press 1988.

McAleese, Dermot, 'Ireland's economic recovery', *Irish Banking Review*, summer 1990, 18–32.

O'Mahony, D., 'Developments in civil aviation in recent years', *Seirbhís Phoiblí*, vol. 9 (1988), no. 3, 17–23.

Stigler, G. (ed.), *Chicago Studies in Political Economy*, Chicago: University of Chicago Press 1988.